Cute Animals to Needle Felt

First published in 2026

Search Press Limited
Wellwood, North Farm Road,
Tunbridge Wells, Kent TN2 3DR

1 2 3 4 5 6 7 8 9 10

Text and templates copyright ©
Roz Dace and Judy Balchin 2026

Styled photography by Stacy Grant
Step-by-step photography by
Mark Davison at Search Press studios
Photographs copyright
© Search Press Ltd. 2026

Photograph of the authors by and copyright
of © Rebecca May Warwick 2026

Design copyright © Search Press Ltd. 2026

ISBN: 978-1-80092-360-7
eBook ISBN: 978-1-80093-344-6

Bookmarked Hub
For further ideas and inspiration, and to join
our free online community, visit
www.bookmarkedhub.com

Publishers' notes
The Publishers and authors can accept no
responsibility for any consequences arising
from the information, advice or instructions
given in this publication.

GPSR information can be found at
www.searchpress.com

Printed in China, TT032026.

Safety notice
These animals are not designed as play toys
and, because of the small parts involved, are
not suitable for children under four years old.

Dedication

For our beautiful daughters Briony, Rebecca and Ruth, who like us live
in crafty worlds where creativity, with all its magic, is a joy and delight.

Acknowledgements

With special thanks to our Search
Press team for their encouragement
and support. In particular, Martin
and Caroline de la Bedoyérè for their
belief in us and helping us reach so
many needle felters everywhere!
With thanks to Phoebe Bowers for
her encouragement and help, our
designer Emma Sutcliffe too, and
our wonderful photographers:
Mark Davison and Stacy Grant.
A huge thank you to our family
and friends for being there, and
to our fantastic social media
followers and students who love what we do and
continue to inspire us with their enthusiasm and sense of fun.

Find us on our website: www.woollyfelters.com

Note on metric and imperial measurements

The projects in this book have been made using metric
measurements, and the imperial equivalents provided
have been calculated following standard conversion
practices. The imperial measurements are often
rounded to the nearest ¼in for ease of use except in
rare circumstances. However, if you need more exact
measurements, there are a number of excellent online
converters that you can use. Always use either metric or
imperial measurements, not a combination of both.

Cute Animals to Needle Felt

20 easy projects

Roz Dace & Judy Balchin

SEARCH PRESS

CONTENTS

Introduction

We are very happy to be sharing the secrets of our amazing craft with you, and we've had great fun creating this treasury of adorable animals. Wool, with its versatility and enduring qualities, is the perfect material for our mini menagerie. With the projects in this book ranging from simple to more complex, you will discover how to capture the texture of the animals: from the furriness of the rabbit and panda, to the smoother contours of the elephant and giraffe.

So, what is needle felting? With a barbed needle and a stabbing motion, the tiny scales on each wool fibre tangle into a 'mass' which can be manipulated into basic, simple shapes. These can then be sculpted and refined into the body parts which make up all of the creatures. We like to call this technique 'creative voodoo'. As the magic works, fluffy fibres are 'transformed' into wonderful woolly creations.

We begin with what you will need, how the techniques work and how to add features, embellishments and colour. The twenty projects subsequently build in skill level, but you can also dip in and out, taking your pick of whichever animal you'd like to make. Once needle felted, the shapes are joined together with a felting needle, and we have provided templates for each shape at the back of the book. There is no sewing or the more messy work of 'wet felting' involved – which is reason enough for us to love this craft! Add a passion for wool and its incredible qualities, and here we are! We have included baby animals too, to show how simple it is to create an enchanting nursery of little ones – simply reduce the size of your templates.

Now, it is time to play. We hope you enjoy your wonderful wool journey and that beginners will love making the simpler creatures. For those of you who have needle felted before, we hope you find the more advanced projects as exciting and as fun as we do.

Happy needle felting!

What you need

We love the fact that needle felting takes up so little working space and it is affordable too. If you are a beginner, you can start with just some wool, a felting pad and a felting needle. Then, if you find you love the magic of the craft, you can have fun adding to your basket of tools, embellishments and treasures.

For those of you who already have wool fibres stashed away, these projects are ideal for using up your leftover wool. Materials can be bought from specialist craft suppliers and they are also readily available online. Everything that you need is included on these pages, or you can simply refer to the materials lists that we have included at the beginning of each project.

Wonderful wool

All the animals are needle felted using coarse wool, which we find is the best for body parts and sculpting. This is because the fibres are normally shorter and thicker, meaning it needle felts faster. The wool is also available in a range of beautiful colours. We use finer Merino wool for details and features. Other types of wool can also be used to embellish the animals, for example in our sheep project we have used small curly Wensleydale locks to cover the body.

Yarn

We have used double knitting (DK/light worsted) wools for some of the tails (see pages 101, 117, 123 and 129). Super fine Angora yarn is also used for Itsy Bitsy Mouse's knitted scarf (see page 89).

Working pad

Needle felting is worked on a soft surface to prevent the needles from breaking. We use a high density foam pad which we cover with hessian (burlap) to prolong its life. There are alternatives available, as shown below, so do explore all options to find out what works best for you.

Foam pad, covered in hessian (burlap)

Felt pad – made up of layers of felted wool

Eco-friendly, rice-filled pad, covered in hessian (burlap)

Coarse wool
Wensleydale locks
Super fine Angora wool
DK (light worsted) yarn
Merino wool

Felting needles

The felting needle is an amazing tool with its shape-making qualities and ability to work fine detail. Different sizes, or gauges, are available either singly or in bulk, and they are categorized by the shapes and thickness of their blades. Remember: the lower the gauge number, the thicker the blade.

- For all of the animals we have used a gauge 40 triangle needle, which is categorized as 'fine' by some suppliers. We normally work on a small scale, and find this size is the most efficient for our projects. If we were making bigger pieces, we would choose to work with a thicker needle.

- A gauge 38 triangle needle has a stronger blade, so we work with it when needle felting within a cookie cutter (see page 45), or near wire (see page 88). A finer needle may break.

- A gauge 38 reverse needle is designed to pull wool fibres out of a felted piece, creating a beautiful fluffy finish – which is fantastic if you want to go 'furry' as we have with Cassandra Panda (see page 107). This needle is also an essential part of our kit.

- Some of our students find the needle difficult to hold, so we advise them to use a single needle holder, which provides a better grip.

- To speed up the felting process, and when making flat shapes, we also use a five-needle felting tool, as shown on page 136 for Cuddly Kangaroo's pouch.

40 TRIANGLE

This needle has a fine, long blade.

38 TRIANGLE

For working near wire or metal.

38 REVERSE

For creating a fluffy finish.

SINGLE NEEDLE HOLDER

This will fit onto all gauges.

FIVE-NEEDLE FELTING TOOL

Can be used on larger, and flat shapes to speed up the felting process.

Storing the needles

The needles are sharp, so it is important to store them safely when you're working with them, and when they are not in use. We keep them in a corner of our pad when working, in needle felted pincushions, or in the felting needle tubes provided by some suppliers. You can also push them into sponge pieces or corrugated card.

Other materials

1. **Autofade pen:** For creating outlines.
2. **Black felt-tip pen:** For colouring Fabulous Fox's ears (see page 49).
3. **Bobble pins:** For marking eye positions.
4. **Bradawl:** To make holes for eyes and tails.
5. **Embellishments:** Such as ribbons, fabric scraps, buttons, miniature crowns, fabric flowers and mini cones.
6. **Embroidery scissors:** For trimming fibres.
7. **Fabric scissors:** For cutting mohair fabric.
8. **Finger guards:** Wear these for protection.
9. **Heart cookie cutter:** To create a heart (see page 45).
10. **Horse hair:** For whiskers.
11. **Mohair fabric:** For Happy Hedgehog (see page 63).
12. **Large eye needle:** For sewing on yarn tails.
13. **Rollerball pen:** For marking hedgehog fabric.
14. **Scalpel:** For scraping pastels into a powder.
15. **Sewing needle:** For adding whiskers.
16. **Sewing pins:** For sewing templates to fabrics.
17. **Small digital scales:** For measuring amounts of wool (optional – see page 15 for advice on measuring wool without scales).
18. **Soft pastels powders, a medium and small paintbrush:** Used to colour features.
19. **Strong clear glue:** For securing eyes, embellishments and Happy Hedgehog's fur (see pages 22 and 63).
20. **Tape measure:** For measuring limbs.
21. **Tweezers:** To remove any broken needles.
22. **Wire:** 1mm (18 gauge) for Itsy Bitsy Mouse's tail (see page 88).
23. **White fabric pen:** For marking darker areas.
24. **Wire-backed black glass eyes:** Available in different sizes from doll- and bear-making suppliers.
25. **Wire cutters:** To cut and trim wire.

Basic techniques

First, get comfortable. Needle felting is not a quick craft, so it is important to sit at the right height with good lighting. If you have never needle felted before, we advise that you read these pages first, have a go and then move on to the delights of choosing your first project.

Holding the needle

Felting needles are sharp, so do take care and take time getting used to the technique. Firstly, it is really important that you hold and use your needle correctly or it will break and if this continues happening you will find the constant replacing expensive. Usually the needle will break in two pieces: the handle and the pointed shaft. Sometimes the shaft will be left embedded in your work. If this happens, use tweezers to extract the needle and dispose of the two parts responsibly.

Finger guards are available should you prefer to use them (see below).

Note: the 40 triangle needle is used throughout this section (pages 14–21).

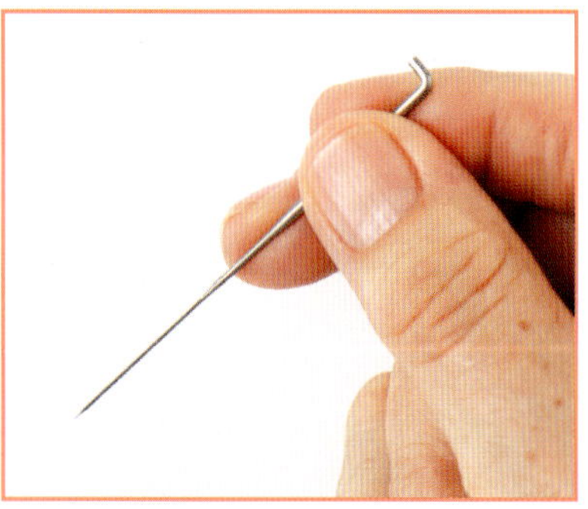

1 Grip the needle firmly with two fingers and a thumb.

2 Always poke the needle in and out at the same angle. Never bend the needle when it is embedded in the wool because it WILL break!

3 Protect the fingers that hold the work with your finger guards.

Grip the handle firmly when using a single or multi-needle tool.

TIP

Felting needles are very sharp. Finger guards are available for protection, but always keep the plasters handy!

Templates

We use templates to make all of the animals, and you will find them at the back of the book – starting from page 138. They are full size and show the sizes and shapes of all of the felted parts that make up each animal. Most of the shapes are 3D but some are needle felted flat: these are labelled as such. Wavy lines show where fibres need to be left, and these are then used to join one shape to another.

We provide wool weights throughout the book so that you can use digital scales to weigh the fibres.

Alternatively, if you do not have scales, you can use the templates as a guide. Wool shrinks by approximately one third when felted. So if you tightly roll the fibres to measure a third larger than the template, they will needle felt down to the right size.

We have included baby animals with every project, to show that by reducing the templates to 80% you can create an adorable nursery of little animals. Always refer to the templates: they are your guide when making all of the projects.

Measuring wool using a template

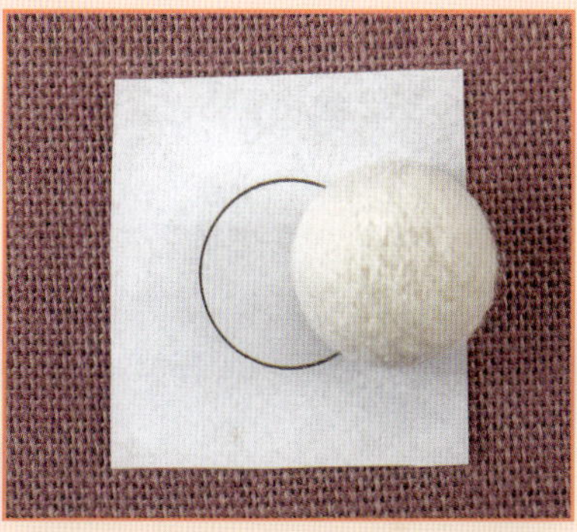

1 Roll the wool tightly one third larger than the template, expelling as much air as possible.

2 Hold the shape firmly. Needle all over using the 40 triangle needle (the shape here is 50% felted).

3 When needled the shape will shrink down to a third to match the template size (fully needle felted piece).

4 Wavy lines on the templates show where to leave loose fibres, and these will be used to join one shape to another (see page 21).

Shapes & features

The stages of needle felting are always the same and this applies to whatever you are making. A repeated stabbing motion with the felting needle will start to bind the loose fibres until a solid shape is formed. The secret to success is to roll the wool tightly when you begin, because if you allow the fibres to spring back to their loose state, you will be needling thin air! Use your dominant hand for stabbing, and the other for turning the wool to achieve an even felt. Follow the steps below to familiarize yourself with the process and have fun watching the magic happen!

Each animal is created using simple 2D and 3D needle felted shapes that are joined together with the felting needle. Different shapes create different animals so the possibilities are endless.

Ball

Balls are good for heads, bodies and bunny tails. The following example uses 5g (¼oz) of wool.

1 Tightly roll the wool into a ball, expelling all of the air.

2 Poke the needle deeply, and evenly, in and around the wool until it retains its shape.

3 Continue until the wool shrinks down and the surface starts to dimple. This shows that the inside of the ball is now needle felted.

4 Roll the ball in your hands. This will speed up the felting process and smooth the surface.

5 Work over the ball with the five-needle tool, then the 40 triangle needle. This will shrink and smooth the fibres more.

6 When the ball matches the template, pin-prick the whole surface with the needle at a slight angle to smooth and tuck in any flyaway fibres.

Oval

Great for a combined body and head shape (for example, for Hootie Owl on page 36). We use them for just bodies too (see Woolly Alpaca on page 92). The following example uses 5g (¼oz) of wool.

1 Lay some wool fibres on the pad, fold in each side, then roll them into a tight, fat sausage.

2 Needle felt one end until it is round and firm. Turn it round and repeat on the other end, working all around the shape.

3 Now follow steps 3–6 for the 'ball' (see pages 16–17). You have finished your oval when it matches the template.

Sausage

Most arms, paws and legs are sausage shapes. The following example uses 2.5g (⅛oz) of wool.

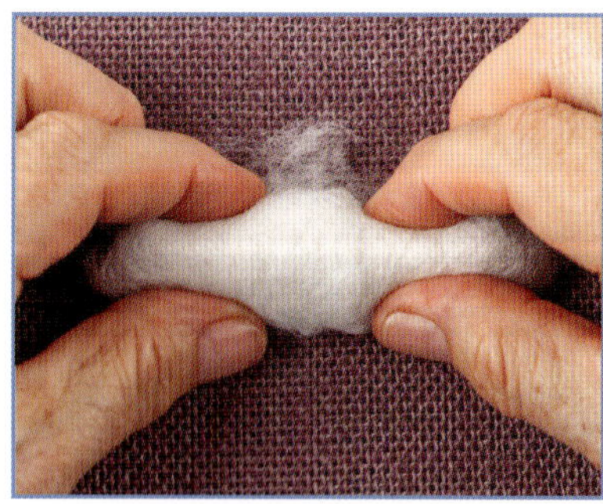

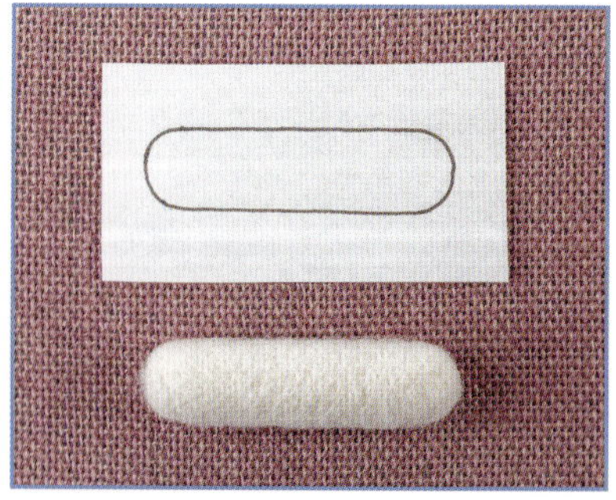

1 Fold the edges of the wool in to neaten, then roll tightly into a sausage.

2 Needle one end until it is rounded, then turn the sausage round and needle the other end to match. Work all around the shape.

3 Now follow steps 3–6 for the 'ball' (see pages 16–17). You have finished when the sausage matches the template.

Cone

A useful shape for animal muzzles, and we also use it for Eliza Hen's beak and tail (see page 67). The following example uses a small amount of wool. Please note, that we leave loose fibres at the base of the cone so they can be attached to a body.

1 Lay the fibres on the pad and fold one end into the middle.

2 Tightly roll the fibres into a cone shape and needle felt the end until it is pointed and firm.

3 Turn the cone round, then with the needle angled towards the point, push and poke the fibres towards the point.

4 The finished cone.

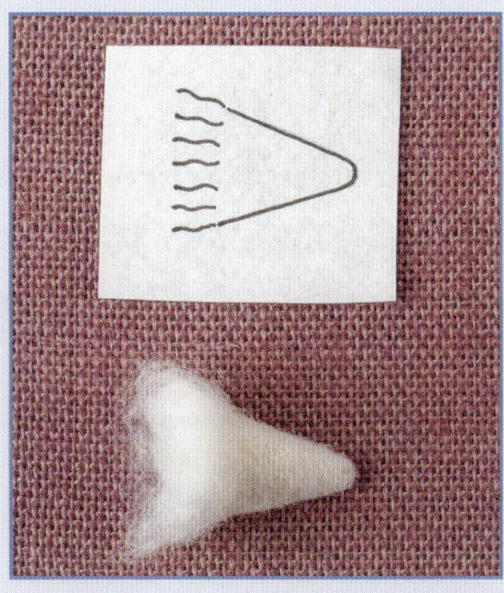

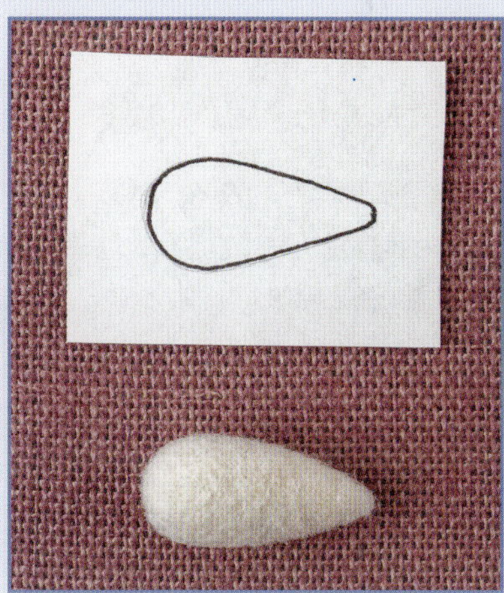

5 Round the end of the cone to create a teardrop matching the size of the template.

Making a flat shape

We use this slightly different technique for ears and wings. There is minimal shrinkage in size apart from the thickness of the pieces. So, lay out the fibres just slightly larger than the templates. Leave loose fibres as shown, so that the shapes can be attached to the head or body. Here, we show how to needle felt an ear.

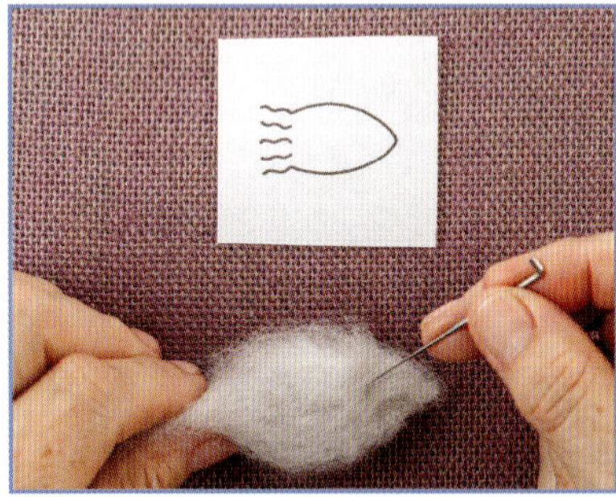

1 Lay some wool fibres on the pad a little larger than the template. Pull them into the template shape with the needle tip, and needle them flat.

2 Peel the ear away and flip it. Needle again, then repeat until the fibres begin to felt.

TIP

You can also use the five-needle tool to speed up the felting process (see the ball technique on pages 16–17 or the Cuddly Kangaroo project on page 136).

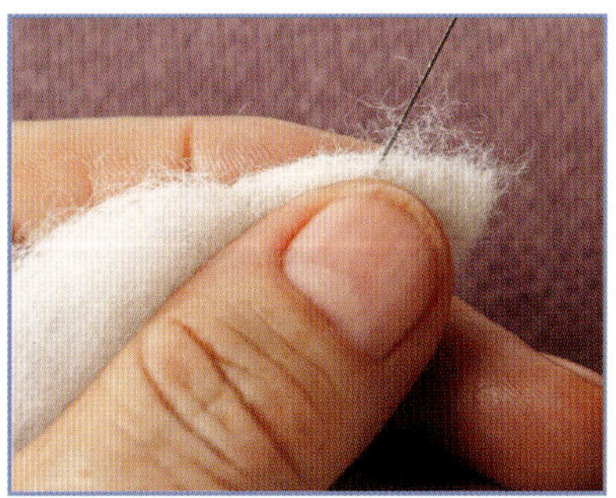

3 When the ear is firm, hold it loosely between your fingers and needle around the edge tucking in any flyaway fibres.

4 Pinch the bottom of the felted ear, and needle into it.

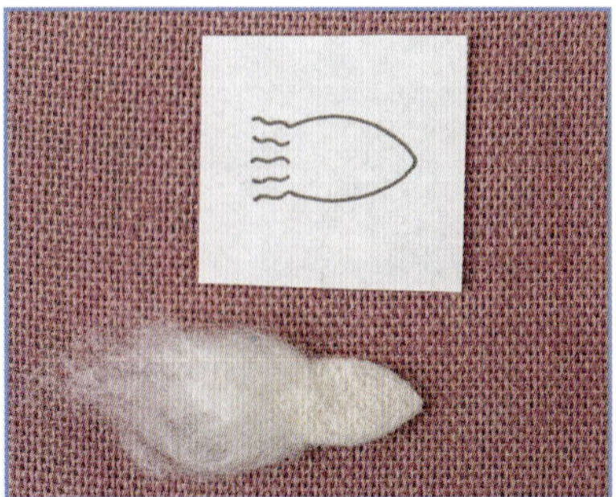

5 The finished ear, with loose fibres left for attaching.

TIP

To neaten the edges you can also use two pieces of card with the wool sandwiched in between them.

Joining shapes

Loose fibres are left when two shapes need to be joined together. These are depicted as wavy lines on the template. Before you start, pull out any bulky loose ends. Note that you will not need many fibres to do the joining!

Make sure, when you join legs to bodies, that your animals can sit or stand correctly before firmly attaching them. If your animal does not sit or stand securely after you have attached the limbs, it is easy to make adjustments. Needle into those areas that need flattening, or add a little wool where needed.

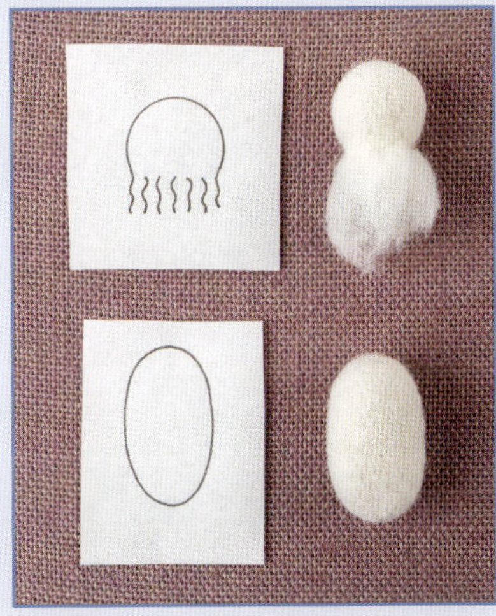

Loose joining fibres are shown as wavy lines on the template.

1 Splay out the loose fibres on the ball.

2 Press the ball onto the oval and needle the fibres in deeply to secure the two shapes.

3 Pin-prick the join all round to create a smooth finish.

Adding features

Different expressions can be achieved with even
slight adjustments to the positioning of features,
so do have a play when adding them.

Eyes

We use wire-backed, glass eyes which are easy to
attach and they add a sparkle of life too! Bobble pins
can help with eye positioning. Move them around to
see how cute you can make your animal look, but do
remove them before needling the eye sockets.

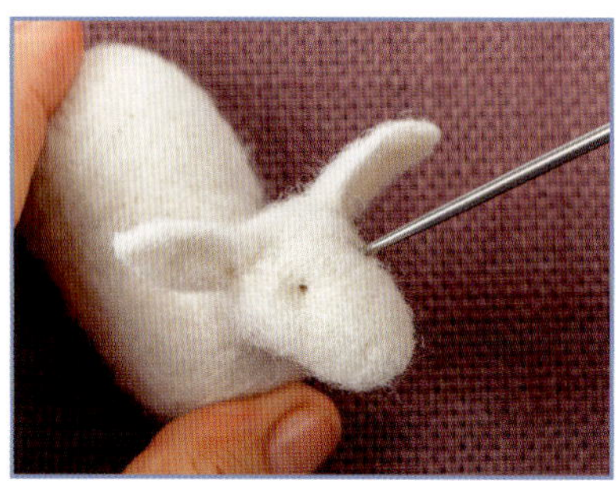

1 Repeatedly needle into one spot to
create an eye socket. Ensure that you
create a smooth dip. Repeat for the
other eye socket.

2 Using a bradawl, make a hole in the
centre of each socket.

3 Glue the end of the eye wires and
push them into the holes.

Noses and mouths

Here, we show a basic technique for adding these features. Other types
of noses and smile lines are shown within the projects. You need only thin
lengths of Merino wool. Using thicker lengths will result in an unrealistic look.

1 Needle the wool into the nose shape.

2 Needle the vertical nose line and add the smile line.
Trim any loose ends.

Adding colour

We use pastels to colour faces and add subtle shading.
A fine powder can be created if some soft pastel is scraped
into a container with a craft knife. This can then be gently
brushed on with a small paintbrush.

Whiskers

Horse hair is strong and looks realistic so it is great for whiskers. Complete
your animal first before sewing them on. Follow steps A–D to attach one set,
then repeat twice more.

A   B   C   D

The finished whiskers!

The PROJECTS

BEFORE YOU START:

1 Unless stated otherwise in the instructions, use a 40 triangle needle.

2 Always work on a needle felting pad, never on a hard surface, or your needles will break.

3 Needle felting is not a quick process. To speed it up, always roll the wool tightly into the required shape before you start stabbing. If you do not, you will be literally needling thin air!

4 Do NOT bend the needle when it is buried in the wool. A 'stab' is not a random action. The needle should go into the wool and come out at the same angle or it will break.

5 Stab the shape evenly, turning it as you work, so that you have an even felt.

6 The initial stabbing should be deep and firm, so that the centre is needle felted as well as the surface. As the shape felts, it will shrink.

7 When the shape is almost template size, you can use the five-needle tool to speed up the process.

8 You can roll any shape in your hands once it is firm to smooth the finish. This will also speed up the felting process.

9 Finally, to smooth the outer surface, pin-prick the shape with slightly angled stabs.

1

Katie Koala

We adore koalas and have adopted Katie and her baby into our woolly family. They love walking on the 'wild' side and eating eucalyptus leaves when they are not sleeping. Just like us, they have their own fingerprints, making each one of them uniquely special.

Finished size

- Katie: 7cm (2¾in) tall
- Baby: 6cm (2¼in) tall

What you need

- Templates for size and shape (see page 138)
- Foam pad
- Five-needle tool
- Felting needle: 40 triangle
- Coarse wool: 18g (¾oz) of beige, a small amount of white and black
- Two 6mm (¼in) wire-backed glass eyes, black
- Autofade pen
- Strong clear glue
- Bradawl
- Embroidery scissors

KATIE'S BABY

Reduce the templates to 80%.
You will need 4mm (³⁄₁₆in)
wire-backed black glass eyes.
When complete, needle a little tuft
of beige wool to the top
of the head.

For this project, refer to the templates on page 138.

1 Head and body Following the instructions on page 18, roll 14g (½oz) of beige wool into a tight oval, and needle all over the shape until it is firm and has reduced to the template size. Then pin-prick the surface until smooth.

2 Needle the bottom flat so your koala will stand firmly.

3 Using an autofade pen, draw an outline for the nose.

4 Features Referring to the template and using a small amount of black wool, needle felt the nose into a domed shape.

5 Attach the eyes (see page 22).

6 Needle a small semi-circle of white wool under the nose for the lower jaw, then add a few white fibres around the eyes.

7 Referring to the template and using a small amount of beige wool for each, needle felt the ears leaving loose fibres (see page 20).

8 Splay out the loose fibres and attach the ears.

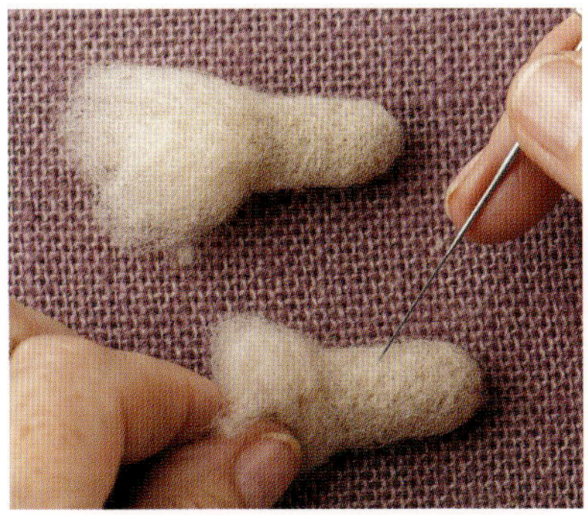

9 Needle a few white fibres into each ear.

10 Arms Roll a small amount of beige wool into a tight sausage and needle one end round. Work up and around the arm until it matches the template, leaving loose ends for attaching. Make two.

11 Splay out the loose fibres, press the arms onto the body and needle them in gently, making sure to curve the arms around the body towards the front. Then needle all round to secure the loose fibres to make a smooth join.

12 Hold the arms against the body and needle into the edges so that they lie snugly against the body.

13 Feet Using a small amount of beige wool for each, needle felt two rounded feet.

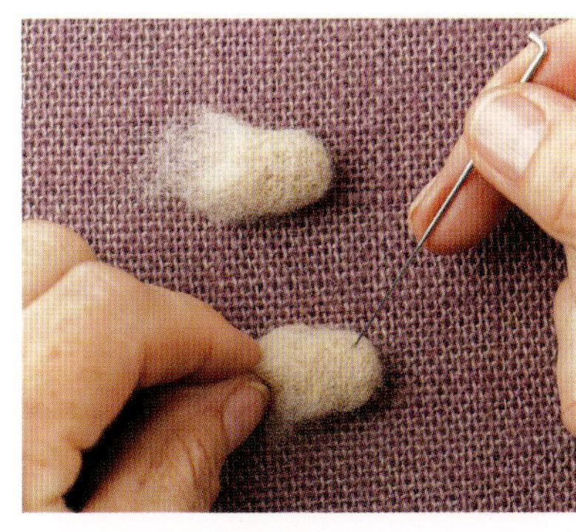

14 Position the feet onto the bottom of the body, and needle up into them, so that they are secure. Make sure that your koala can stand. (If there is still a wobble, add a little extra wool to your koala's bottom.)

2

Pippin Penguin

These little penguins are looking forward to lots of woolly adventures with you. Friendly and fun, they love swimming, tobogganing and ice skating and will make cool companions!

Finished size

- Pippin: 8cm (3in) tall
- Baby: 6cm (2¼in) tall

What you need

- Templates for size and shape (see page 138)
- Foam pad
- Five-needle tool
- Felting needle: 40 triangle
- Coarse wool: 16g (⅝oz) black, 4g (⅛oz) white, 3g (⅛oz) orange
- Two 8mm (⁵⁄₁₆in) wire-backed glass eyes, black
- Pink pastel powder and a small paintbrush
- Small gold crown: 17mm (½in) diameter
- White fabric pen
- Strong clear glue
- Bradawl
- Embroidery scissors

PIPPIN'S BABY
Reduce the templates to 80%.
You will need two 4mm (³⁄₁₆in)
wire-backed, black glass eyes. To finish off,
needle a small tuft of black wool to the top
of the baby's head.

For this project, refer to the templates on page 138.

1 Head and body Following the instructions on page 18, roll 14g (½oz) of black wool into a tight oval and needle all over until it is firm and has reduced to the template size.

2 Needle the bottom flat, making sure that your penguin will stand firmly.

3 Using the white marking pen, draw on the face and chest shape.

4 Fill in the area with 4g (⅛oz) of white wool, needling the fibres so they are secure.

5 Pin-prick the area with slightly angled stabs to smooth and neaten.

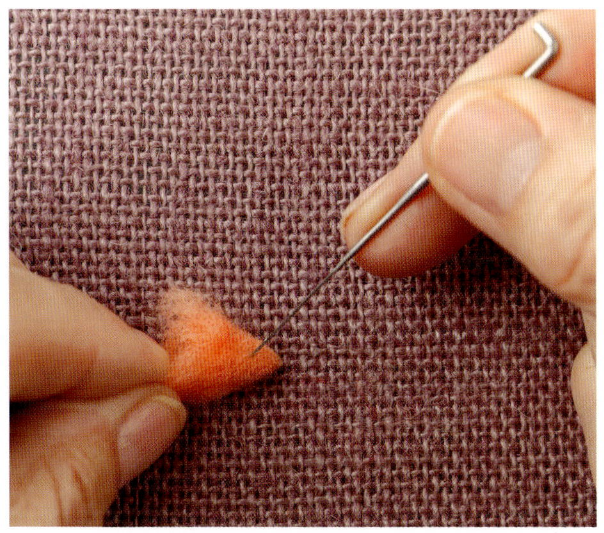 

6 Roll a small orange cone for the beak and needle felt one end into a small point, leaving loose fibres at the other end for attaching.

7 Splay out the fibres, press the beak onto the face and needle the fibres in, attaching the beak firmly.

8 Attach the eyes (see page 22).

9 Needle a little white wool into two small soft sausages, and gently attach them above each eye to create brows.

10 Wings Referring to the template and using 2g (¹⁄₁₆oz) of black wool for each, needle felt two flat wings (see page 20). Leave loose fibres for attaching.

11 Splay out the fibres, press the wings onto the body and needle the loose fibres in smoothly and firmly (see page 21).

12 Feet Using a small amount of orange wool for each, needle felt two feet until they match the template.

13 Glue them to the bottom of the body and needle any loose fibres in.

14 Tail Referring to the template and using a small amount of black wool, needle felt the tail. Leave loose fibres.

15 Needle the loose fibres into the body, so that the tail supports the penguin and helps him to stand firmly.

16 Features Lightly brush the cheeks with a little pink pastel powder and crown your King Pippin!

3

Hootie Owl

Our dear little woolly owls are normally nocturnal and known for their wise ways. This simple design will allow you to learn how to create character and cuteness, while practising the basics.

Finished size

- Hootie: 7cm (2¾in) tall
- Baby: 5cm (2in) tall

What you need

- Templates for size and shape (see page 138)
- Foam pad
- Five-needle tool
- Felting needle: 40 triangle
- Coarse wool: approximately 17g (⅝oz) beige, 3g (⅛oz) white, 2g (¹⁄₁₆oz) rust
- Merino wool: a small amount of brown
- Two 8mm (⁵⁄₁₆in) wire-backed glass eyes, black
- Autofade pen
- Strong clear glue
- Bradawl
- Embroidery scissors

HOOTIE'S
FLEDGLING
Reduce the templates to 80%.
You will need 6mm (¼in) wire-backed
black glass eyes.

For this project, refer to the templates on page 138.

1 Head and body Following the instructions on page 18, roll 14g (½oz) of beige wool into a tight oval and needle all over until it is firm and has reduced to the template size, then pin-prick the surface to smooth.

2 Needle the bottom flat so the owl will stand firmly.

3 Draw the face and chest outline on using an autofade pen.

4 Fill in these areas with 3g (⅛oz) of white wool, needling the fibres so they are secure and cover the beige wool completely.

5 For the beak, needle a small amount of rust wool into the space between the eyes to create a raised spot.

6 Attach the eyes (see page 22).

7 Referring to the template and using a small amount of beige wool for each, needle felt the ears, leaving loose fibres.

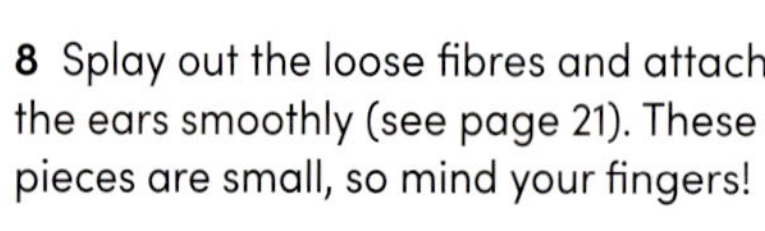

8 Splay out the loose fibres and attach the ears smoothly (see page 21). These pieces are small, so mind your fingers!

9 Wings Referring to the template and using a small amount of beige wool for each, needle felt two rounded wings. The upper sides should be domed, and the undersides should be flat. Leave loose fibres for attaching.

10 Apply a little glue to each flat side and press them onto the body. Needle in the loose fibres, and around the edges of the wings.

11 Feet Using a small amount of rust wool for each, needle felt the feet.

12 Attach the feet to the bottom of the body. Needle up into them and the body, to secure. Make sure that your owl can stand.

13 Needle small wisps of brown Merino wool into the chest to suggest feathers. Trim away any flyaway fibres to give a smooth finish.

4

Bonny Bunny

Sociable, intelligent, with a love of carrots and adventures, our fluffy little bunny is a delight! Her heart is made using a cookie cutter. This is a simple yet effective way to create accessories for any of the projects.

Finished size

- Bonny: 11cm (4¼in) tall
- Baby: 9cm (3½in) tall

What you need

- Templates for size and shape (see page 138)
- Foam pad
- Felting needles: 40 triangle, 38 triangle, 38 reverse
- Five-needle tool
- Coarse wool: 20g (¾oz) white, a small amount of red, a small amount of pink
- Merino wool: a small amount of black
- Two 4mm (³⁄₁₆in) wire-backed glass eyes, black
- Sewing needle
- White horse hair for whiskers
- Cookie cutter: heart-shaped 2.5cm (1in) wide
- Pink pastel powder and a small paint brush
- Strong clear glue
- Bradawl
- Embroidery scissors

BONNY'S BABY
Reduce the templates to 80%. You
will need 3mm (⅛in) wire-backed black
glass eyes. We have used beige wool with a
few white fibres needled into the chest, and
given the baby bunny
a small fabric flower.

1 Head and body Following the instructions on page 18, roll 14g (½oz) of white wool into a tight oval and needle all over until it is firm and has reduced to the template size, then pin-prick the surface to smooth.

2 Needle the bottom flat so your bunny will stand firmly.

3 Referring to the template and using a small amount of white wool for both ears, needle felt the shapes leaving loose fibres (see page 20).

4 Splay out the loose fibres, press one ear into place and needle the loose fibres into the head. Pin-prick the surface to smooth the join. Repeat for the other ear.

5 Fold one ear down and needle into the fold to secure it.

6 For the muzzle lay out a small amount of white wool, then gently needle into the centre to form it into a soft 'pad'. Leave loose fibres around the edge.

7 Lay the muzzle 'pad' onto the face, then pin-prick the loose fibres in smoothly.

8 Features Using thin wisps of pink wool, needle the nose in.

9 Repeatedly needle into the eye socket areas to create dips, and attach the eyes (see page 22), pushing them firmly into the muzzle.

10 Using a wisp of black Merino wool, needle a small vertical line from the bottom of the nose down. Divide the wisp in two and needle each length into a smile line. Trim any ends to neaten.

11 Feet Referring to the template and using a small amount of white wool for each, needle felt the feet.

12 Splay out the loose fibres and needle through the feet and up into the body, to secure. Make sure that your bunny will stand without falling over.

13 Tail Using a small amount of white wool, needle a small soft ball and gently needle it into the bunny's lower back. This will help the bunny stand up!

14 For the arms use a small amount of white wool for each. Roll a tight sausage, needle one end round, then work up and around the arm until it matches the template. Leave loose ends for attaching. Repeat for the second arm.

15 Splay out the loose fibres and attach the arms (see page 21).

16 Heart Using a cookie cutter, make a heart: place the cutter on the pad and fill it with a small amount of red wool. Using the 38 triangle needle, needle the fibres into the cutter so that they flatten and start to felt.

17 Lift the cutter and gently peel the heart from the pad. Turn both the cutter and heart over and repeat until the fibres are firm. Remove the cutter. Continue needling the heart, pointing the needle towards the centre. Turn it several times to felt both sides.

18 Glue the heart between the paws. Then, lightly brush a little pink pastel powder onto the cheeks and inner ears.

19 Sew three sets of whiskers into the face (see page 23).

20 Using the reverse needle, work over the head and body to create a fluffy look. Trim back any longer fibres.

5

Fabulous Fox

In folklore foxes are said to be cunning and playful, while in some cultures they are thought to be a good omen. We love our woolly foxes for their craftiness of course!

Finished size

- Fox: 8cm (3in) tall
- Cub: 5.5cm (2¼in) tall

What you need

- Templates for size and shape (see page 139)
- Foam pad
- Felting needle: 40 triangle
- Five-needle tool
- Coarse wool: approximately 18g (½oz) of rust, 3g (¼oz) of white
- Merino wool: a small amount of black
- Two 5mm (¼in) wire-backed glass eyes, black
- Thick black felt-tip pen
- White fabric pen
- Black horse hair for whiskers
- Sewing needle
- Strong clear glue
- Bradawl
- Embroidery scissors

FOX CUB
Reduce the templates to 80%.
You will need 2mm (1⁄16in)
wire-backed, black glass eyes.

1 Head and body Following the instructions on page 18, roll 14g (½oz) of rust wool into a tight oval and needle all over until it is firm and has reduced to the template size, then pin-prick the surface to smooth.

2 Needle the bottom flat so your fox will stand firmly.

3 Referring to the template and using a small amount of rust wool, roll a cone for the muzzle (see page 19). Needle the nose end into a point. Work around the cone leaving loose fibres at the thicker end for attaching.

4 Splay out the fibres, press the muzzle onto the face and needle the loose fibres in smoothly and firmly (see page 21).

5 Using a small amount of rust wool for each, needle felt the ears leaving loose fibres (see page 20).

6 Attach the ears (see page 21).

7 Gently needle white wool into the inner ears.

8 Draw a black line around the edges with a felt-tip pen.

9 Attach the eyes (see page 22).

10 Using the white fabric pen, draw the outline of your fox's white chest area.

11 Now fill the outlined area with 2g (1⁄16oz) of white wool, needling the fibres so they are secure. Cover the rust wool completely.

12 Pull out thin wisps of black Merino wool and needle a small nose triangle into the face.

13 Needle a small vertical line from the bottom of the nose downwards, and needle the smile lines. Trim to neaten.

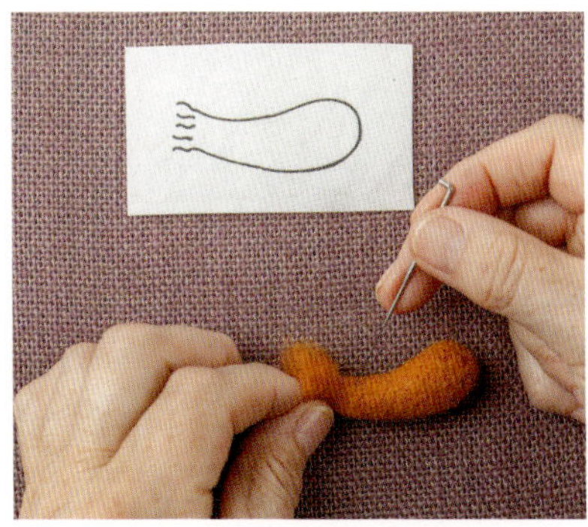

14 Tail Referring to the template, roll a small amount of wool into a tight sausage and needle the end round. Continue needle felting the sausage so that it bends slightly and narrows at the end, leaving loose ends for attaching.

15 Needle felt a small amount of white wool into the end of the tail, creating a slight point.

16 Attach the tail so that it follows the curve of the body, then glue it in place. To further secure it, needle the fibres in smoothly and firmly.

17 Feet Referring to the template and using a small amount of rust wool for each, needle felt the feet. Glue them on and needle up into them, to secure. Make sure that your fox can stand upright.

18 Attach three sets of black whiskers (see page 23).

#6

Timmy Guinea Pig

These cuddly, sociable little animals thrive on love and companionship – they spend their days sharing life's pleasures with their family and friends! In many cultures guinea pigs represent peace, harmony and the warmth of togetherness.

Finished size

- Timmy: 5cm (2in) tall, 8cm (3in) long
- Pup: 3cm (1¼in) tall, 6cm (2¼in) long

What you need

- Templates for size and shape (see page 139)
- Foam pad
- Felting needle: 40 triangle
- Five-needle tool
- Coarse wool: 16g (½oz) white, 6g (¼oz) rust
- Merino wool: a small amount of black and pink
- Autofade pen
- Two 6mm (¼in) wire-backed glass eyes, black
- Strong clear glue
- Bradawl
- Embroidery scissors

TIMMY'S PUP

Reduce the templates to 80%.
You will need 4mm (³⁄₁₆in) wire-backed
black glass eyes. We have added two black
patches to our pup, giving this little one its
own cute markings!

1 Head and body Following the instructions on page 18, roll 14g (½oz) of white wool into a tight oval and needle all over until it is firm and has reduced to the template size.

2 For the nose area, lay down a small circle of white wool. Work towards the centre from the outside, with the needle held at a shallow angle. Form the wool into a firm pad with loose fibres all round.

3 Lay the pad on one end of the oval, and needle the fibres in, pin-pricking at a slight angle to smooth the join.

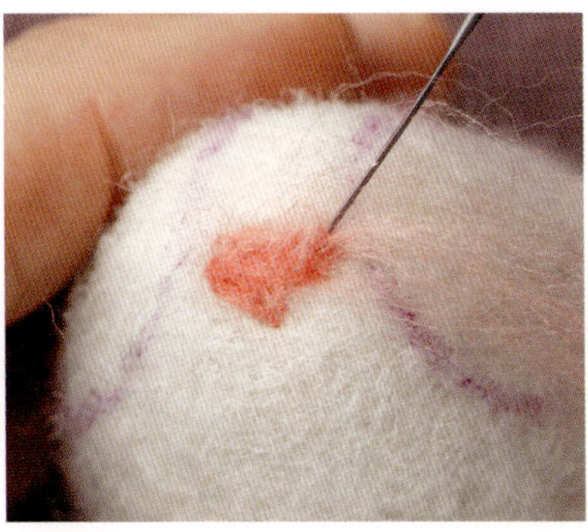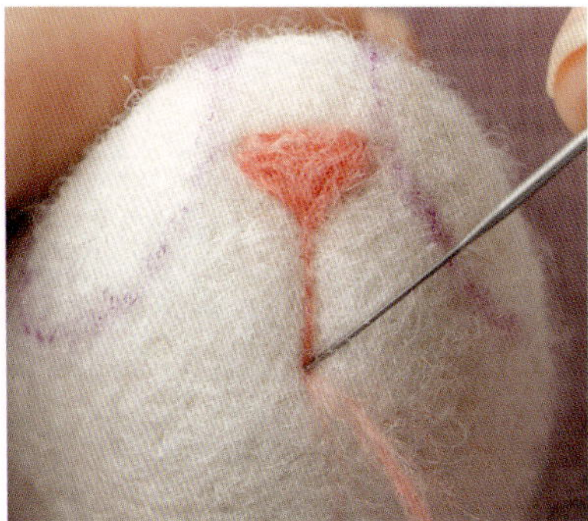

4 Using an autofade pen, draw on the nose, eye patches and the line around the body.

5 Needle in the triangular nose using thin wisps of pink Merino wool.

6 Needle a pink vertical line below the nose.

7 For the bottom lip, needle a small ball and attach it below the vertical pink line.

8 Using a thin wisp of black Merino wool, needle in the mouth line.

9 Using approximately 4g (⅛oz) of rust wool, fill in the back area of the body and the two eye patches.

10 Referring to the template and using a small amount of rust wool for both ears, needle felt the ears leaving loose fibres.

11 Attach each ear to a patch (see page 21).

12 Attach the eyes (see page 22).

13 Bend the ears forwards, and needle into the folds to secure.

14 Legs Roll a tight sausage using a small amount of white wool, then needle one of the ends round.

15 Referring to the template, needle along and around the sausage, before bending the wool upwards. Needle into the bend to create a heel. Make another leg using white wool and two with rust. Leave loose fibres.

16 Splay out the fibres and attach the two white front legs and two rust back legs. Needle the loose ends in firmly and smoothly.

7

Happy Hedgehog

Hedgehogs can be found in a range of different habitats including parks, forests and even deserts. The habitats around our homes offer them refuge and food too, and they are often referred to as a gardener's 'best friend'. Since they are known for their protective quills, we have chosen to give our little hedgehogs fabric mohair coats, to replicate a 'spiky' effect.

Finished size

- Hedgehog: 8cm (3in) tall, 9.5cm (3¾in) long
- Hoglet: 4.5cm (1¾in) tall, 6cm (2¼in) long

What you need

- Templates for size and shape (see page 139)
- Foam pad
- Felting needle: 40 triangle
- Five-needle tool
- Coarse wool: 17g (⅝oz) beige, a small amount of white
- Merino wool: a small amount of black
- Mohair fabric: 11cm (4¼in) square
- Two 6mm (¼in) wire-backed glass eyes, in black
- Brown and pink pastel powders and a small paintbrush
- Black rollerball pen
- Strong clear glue
- Bradawl
- Embroidery scissors
- Fabric cutting scissors
- Sewing pins

HOGLET
Reduce the templates to 80%.
You will need 4mm (³⁄₁₆in)
wire-backed black glass eyes.
Our little hoglet is perfect as he is – we
have not added any feet.

1 Head and body Following the instructions on page 18, roll 14g (½oz) of beige wool into a tight oval and needle all over the shape until it is firm and has reduced to the template size.

2 Needle the bottom flat so your hedgehog will stand firmly.

3 For the snout, lay a small amount of beige wool on the pad. Following the instructions on page 19, needle a cone. Leave loose ends for attaching.

4 Splay out the fibres, press the snout onto the body, then needle the loose ends smoothly and firmly to secure it into the head (see page 21).

5 Features Using thin wisps of black Merino wool, needle in the nose.

6 Needle in the smile line using a wisp of black Merino wool.

7 Attach the eyes (see page 22).

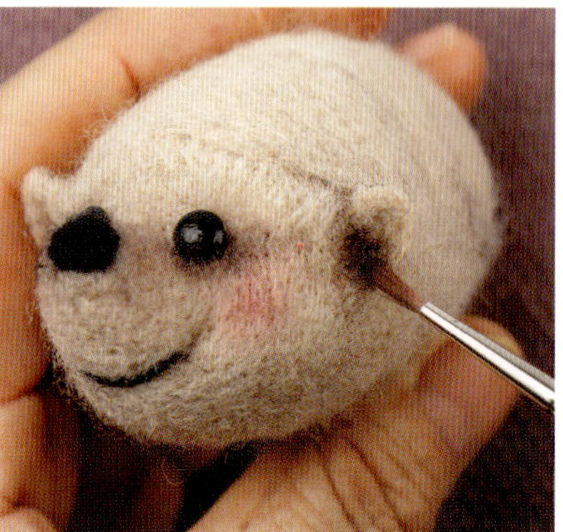

8 Referring to the template and using a small amount of beige wool for both ears, needle felt the ears leaving loose fibres.

9 Attach the ears (see page 21).

10 Brush a little pink pastel powder onto the cheeks, then lightly brush a little brown onto the nose and inner ears.

11 Legs Referring to the template, roll a tight sausage using a small amount of beige wool, then needle the end round for the foot. Bend the wool up to create a heel, and needle into the fold to secure the fibres. Leave loose fibres for attaching. Make four.

12 Splay out the loose fibres, press one leg onto the body and needle the fibres in smoothly. Repeat for the other three legs.

13 Referring to the template, trace the fabric outline onto paper, cut it out and pin it to the back of the mohair fabric. Draw around it with a black rollerball pen.

14 Cut out the shape, spread glue over the back, then press it onto the hedgehog's body.

15 Needle a little white wool around the edge of the fabric and to the underbelly to soften the join.

8

Eliza Hen

It is said that hens make a 'purring' sound when they are feeling comfortable and safe. Mother hens also chirp to their chicks while they are still eggbound, with the little ones chirping a reply. These smart birds have great memories too, and it is known that they pass on their knowledge to their friends and family. Eliza and her chick are looking for someone to love, and they would be happy to find a good home where they can play and have fun.

Finished size

- Eliza: 9cm (3½in) tall, 7cm (2¾) wide
- Chick: 6cm (2¼in) tall, 5cm (2in) wide

What you need

- Templates for size and shape (see page 140)
- Foam pad
- Felting needle: 40 triangle
- Five-needle tool
- Coarse wool: 20g (¾oz) light brown, 2g (¼oz) red, a small amount of orange, 2g (¼oz) mixed yellow and rust for the nest
- Two 4mm (³⁄₁₆in) wire-backed glass eyes, black
- Orange pastel powder and a medium paintbrush
- Strong clear glue
- Bradawl
- Embroidery scissors

ELIZA'S CHICK
Reduce the templates to 80% and use yellow wool. You will need 2mm (1⁄16in) black wire-backed eyes. Do not add the comb and wattles. When finished, lightly dust the head and wings with yellow pastel powder and add a fluffy tuft of wool onto the top of the head.

For this project, refer to the templates on page 140.

1 Body Following the instructions on page 18, roll 14g (½oz) of light brown wool into a tight oval and needle all over until it is firm and has reduced to the template size. Then pin-prick the surface until smooth.

2 Needle the bottom flat so your hen will sit firmly.

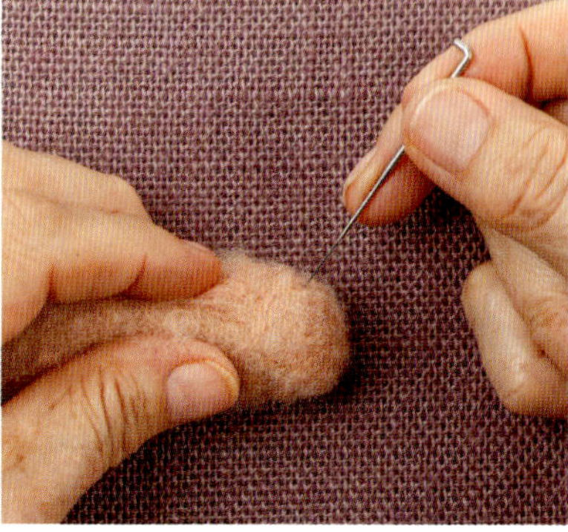

3 Head Roll 3.5g (⅛oz) of light brown wool into a tight sausage (see page 18) and needle the end until round.

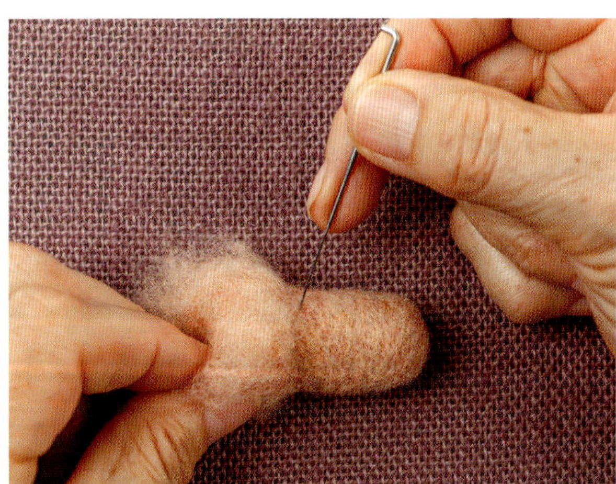

4 Referring to the template, continue needle felting the sausage to create the neck, leaving loose fibres for attaching.

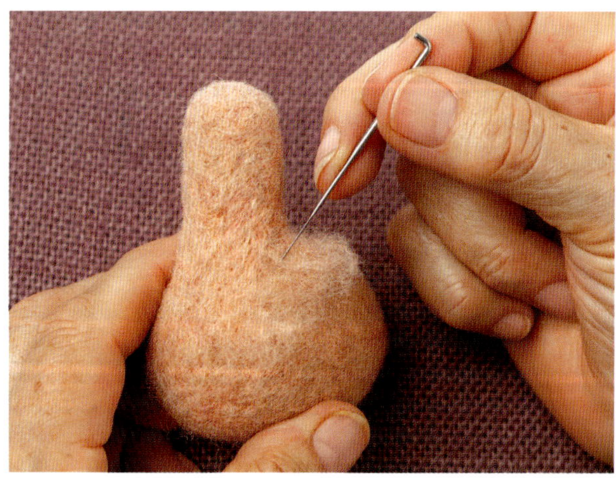

5 Splay out the neck fibres, press the head onto the body and needle the ends in for a smooth finish.

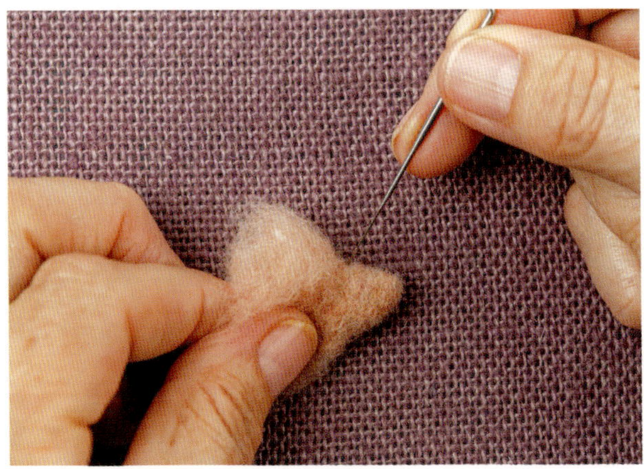

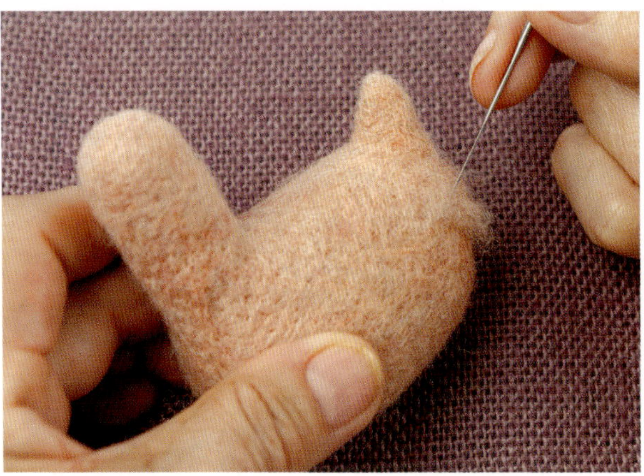

6 Tail Using a small amount of light brown wool, needle felt a cone. Leave loose fibres for attaching (see page 19).

7 Splay out the loose fibres and attach the tail to the body smoothly and firmly.

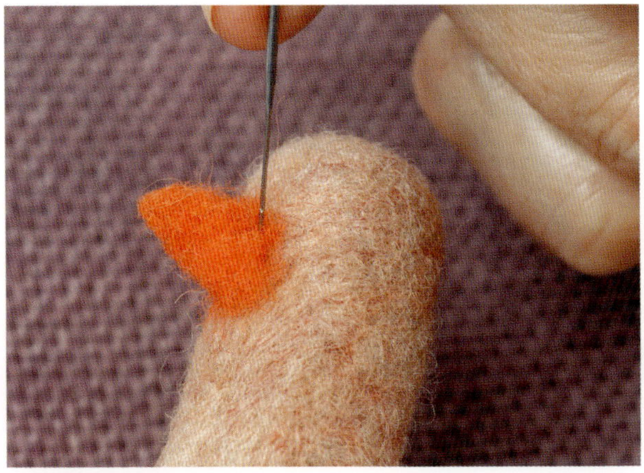

8 Features Needle felt a small orange cone for the beak and attach it to the head.

9 Attach the eyes (see page 22).

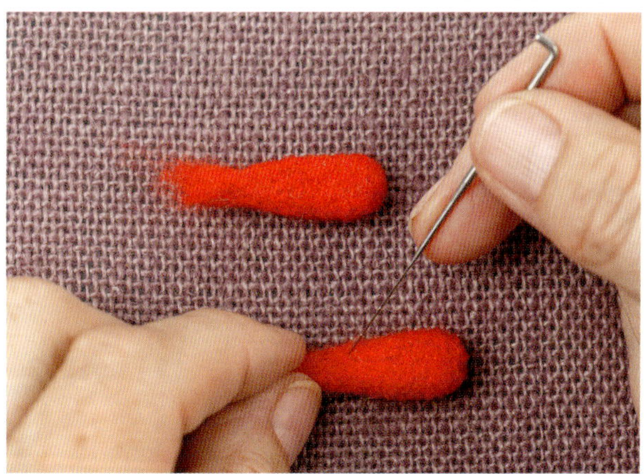

10 Referring to the template and using a small amount of red wool for each, needle felt two wattles leaving loose fibres.

11 Attach the wattles beneath the beak.

12 Using small amounts of red wool for each, needle felt three teardrop shapes.

13 Attach the teardrops to the top of the head: these form the comb.

14 Wings Using a small amount of light brown wool for each, needle felt two wings until they match the template. Create scalloped edges on both wings, and leave loose fibres for attaching.

15 Splay out the loose fibres, and press the wings onto the body. Needle them in smoothly and firmly.

16 Using a medium paintbrush, lightly colour the head, tail and ends of the wings with orange pastel powder.

17 Nest Mix 2g (1/16oz) of yellow and orange wool, arrange the fibres into a circle shape measuring 9cm (3½in) in diameter, and needle the fibres lightly to create a fluffy nest.

18 Finally, place Eliza on top of her nest!

9

Snuggly Sheep

Where would we be without sheep? We love wool, so we had to include this sweet and snuggly family. Wensleydale locks are needled into their bodies, and if you angle their heads when you attach them, this makes them look even cuter!

Finished size

- Sheep: 7.5cm (3in) tall, 9cm (3½in) long
- Lamb: 5cm (2in) tall, 7cm (2¾in) long
- Teeny lamb: 4cm (1½in) tall, 5cm (2in) long

What you need

- Templates for size and shape (see page 140)
- Foam pad
- Felting needle: 40 triangle
- Five-needle tool
- Coarse wool: approximately 18g (¾oz) white
- Merino wool: a small amount of black
- Wensleydale locks: 4g (⅛oz) natural white
- Two 4mm (³⁄₁₆in) wire-backed glass eyes, black
- Pink pastel powder and a small paintbrush
- Strong clear glue
- Bradawl
- Embroidery scissors

LAMBS

Reduce the templates to 80% (or 50% if you are making the teeny lamb). You will need 2mm and 1mm (1/16in) wire-backed black glass eyes for both. Glue colourful ribbon bows of your choice onto the lambs.

For this project, refer to the templates on page 140.

1 Body Following the instructions on page 18, roll 14g (½oz) of wool into a tight oval and needle all over until it is firm and has reduced to the template size.

2 Head Referring to the template, roll 2.5g (⅛oz) of wool into a tight sausage and needle felt the end round.

3 To create the neck, bend the wool down and needle into the bend.

4 Splay out the loose fibres and press the head onto the body angling the head slightly up and to one side, then needle them in firmly (see page 21).

5 Referring to the template and using a small amount of wool for both ears, needle felt them leaving loose fibres.

6 Splay out the loose fibres and attach the ears (see page 21).

7 Features Attach the eyes (see page 22).

8 Using thin wisps of black Merino wool, needle in the nose and mouth (see page 22).

9 Lightly brush the nose, inner ears and cheeks with pink pastel powder.

10 Cover the body with Wensleydale locks, leaving underneath uncovered.

11 Finally, needle lengths of Wensleydale locks into the head, and around the face.

Cozy Cat

If you love cats, this simple project is a great way to learn how to needle felt. Use the colours shown here, or recreate your own pet. The cuteness is captured in the features, so do play around and try out different expressions.

Finished size

- Cat: 11cm (4¼in) tall, 8.5cm (3¼in) long
- Kitten: 7.5cm (3in) tall, 6cm (2¼in) long

What you need

- Templates for size and shape (see page 140)
- Foam pad
- Felting needle: 40 triangle
- Five-needle tool
- Coarse wool: 17g (½oz) white, 6g (¼oz) peach
- Merino wool: a small amount of pink and black
- Two 6mm (¼in) wire-backed glass eyes, black
- Autofade pen
- White horse hair for whiskers
- Sewing needle
- Strong clear glue
- Bradawl
- Embroidery scissors

KITTEN
Reduce the templates to 80%.
You will need 6mm (¼in) wire-backed
glass eyes. To make the eyes stand out
against black wool, needle a little white wool
behind each eye.

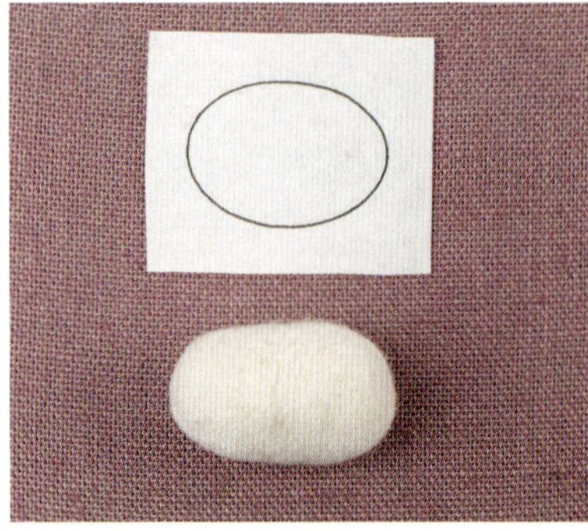

1 Head and body Following the instructions on page 18, roll 14g (½in) of wool into a tight oval and needle all over until it is firm and has reduced to the template size.

2 Pull out thin lengths of pink Merino wool and needle in the triangular nose.

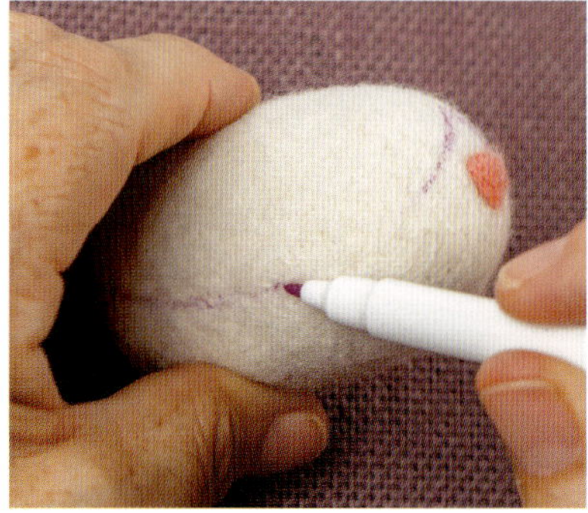

3 Using an autofade pen, outline the upper body area.

4 Fill this in with 3g (⅛oz) of peach wool, needling the fibres so that they are secure and cover the white wool completely. Pin-prick all over the body with slightly angled shallow stabs to smooth and neaten.

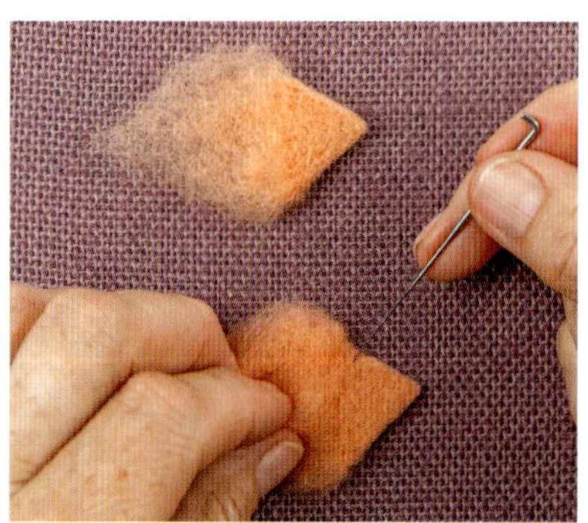

5 Using small amounts of peach wool, needle felt the ears leaving loose fibres (see page 20).

6 Splay out the loose fibres, press them onto the head and needle them in smoothly and firmly.

7 Using wisps of black Merino wool, needle in the mouth.

8 Attach the eyes (see page 22).

9 Legs Referring to the template, roll a small amount of white wool into a tight sausage, then needle one end round. Needle up the rest of the sausage leaving loose fibres for attaching. Make four.

10 Splay out the fibres and press one leg onto the body. Needle the fibres in smoothly and firmly. Repeat for the other three legs.

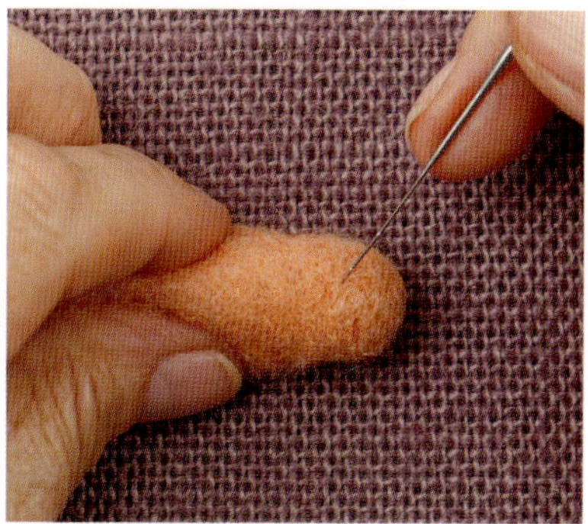

11 Tail Referring to the template, roll a small amount of peach wool into a tight sausage, then needle one end round.

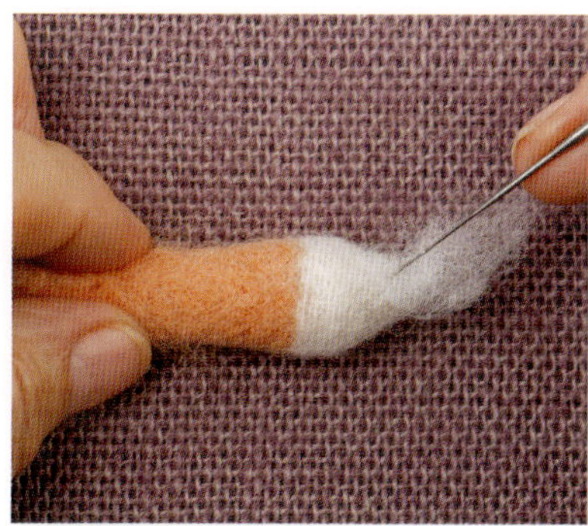

12 Needle the sausage, narrowing it as you work. Leave loose fibres for attaching. When the tail is firm, cover the end with white wool.

13 Attach the tail, needling the loose fibres in smoothly and firmly.

14 Attach the whiskers (see page 23).

11

Waggy Dog

Just like us, dogs want to be loved – especially our woolly ones!
They make great companions, and this project can be adapted
to represent your own pet. If you want a cuter, more inquisitive look,
tilt the head slightly to one side, and slightly upwards.

Finished size

- Dog: 10cm (4in) tall, 8cm (3in) long
- Puppy: 8cm (3in) tall, 6.5cm (2½in) long

What you need

- Templates for size and shape (see page 140)
- Foam pad
- Felting needle: 40 triangle
- Five-needle tool
- Coarse wool: 20g (¾oz) white, 6g (¼oz) brown
- Merino wool: a small amount of black
- Two 5mm (¼in) wire-backed glass eyes, black
- Autofade pen
- Strong clear glue
- Bradawl
- Embroidery scissors

PUPPY
Reduce the templates to 80%. You will need 3mm (⅛in) wire-backed black glass eyes. Different colours could be used, and patches added too.

1 Head and body Following the instructions on page 18, roll 14g (½oz) of white wool into a tight oval, and needle all over the shape until it is firm and has reduced to the template size.

2 Referring to the template, needle felt the muzzle using a small amount of wool. Roll a tight sausage and needle all round leaving loose fibres for attaching.

3 Splay out the fibres and press it onto the end of the body. Needle the loose fibres in smoothly and firmly (see page 21).

4 Using thin wisps of black Merino wool, needle the nose triangle into the end of the muzzle.

5 Needle in the mouth details.

6 Draw in the outline of the brown upper body using the autofade pen.

7 Fill in this area with approximately 4g (⅛oz) of brown wool, needling the fibres so they are secure and cover the white wool completely. Pin-prick at a slight angle to smooth and neaten.

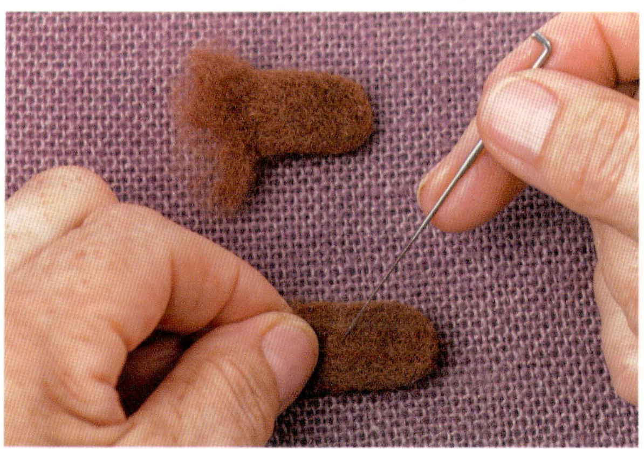

8 Referring to the template and using a small amount of brown wool for both, needle felt the ears leaving loose fibres.

9 Splay out the fibres and needle them into the top of the head firmly and smoothly (see page 21).

10 Bend each ear down and needle into the folds to secure them.

11 Needle repeatedly into the head to create shallow dips for the eye sockets. Attach the eyes (see page 22).

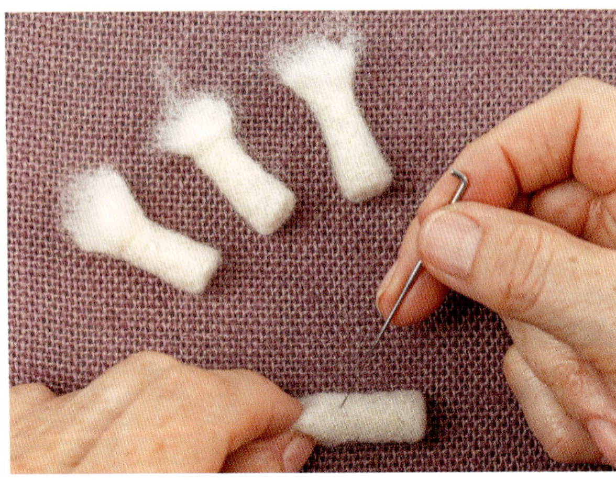

12 Legs Referring to the template and using a small amount of white wool for each leg, roll a tight sausage, then needle one end flat. Needle up and around the leg leaving loose fibres for attaching. Make four.

13 Splay out the loose fibres, press one leg on the body and needle the fibres in firmly and smoothly. Repeat for the other three legs.

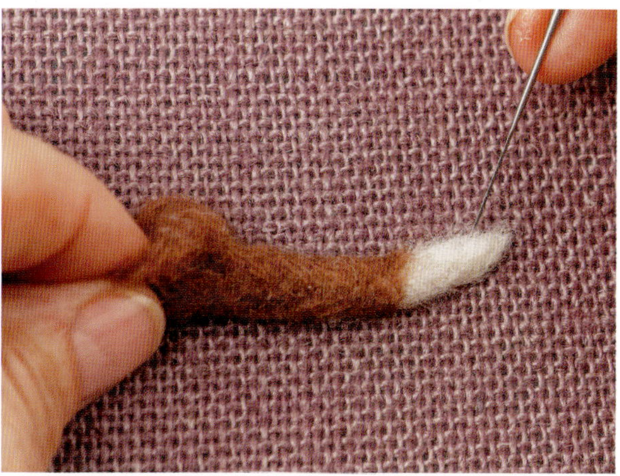

14 Tail Referring to the template and using a small amount of brown wool, roll the fibres into a tight sausage leaving loose fibres at one end.

15 When the tail is firm, needle white wool into the tip.

16 To finish your 'waggy' dog, attach the tail.

12

Itsy Bitsy Mouse

Cute, charming and lovable, these little companions are fun to make.
The head and body are made separately, then joined, and the tail is wired
so that it can be posed.

Finished size

- Itsy Bitsy: 9.5cm (3¾in) tall
- Baby: 8cm (3in) tall

What you need

- Templates for size and shape (see page 141)
- Foam pad
- Five-needle tool
- Felting needles: 40 triangle, 38 triangle
- Coarse wool: 19g (¾oz) beige wool, a small amount of white
- Merino wool: a small amount of pink and black
- Two 3mm (⅛in) wire-backed glass eyes, black
- Wire: 6cm (2¼in) length of 1mm (18 gauge) wire
- White horse hair for whiskers
- Sewing needle
- Pink pastel powder and a small paintbrush
- Strong clear glue
- Bradawl
- Embroidery scissors
- Mini pine cone
- 3mm (UK 11, US 2/3) knitting needles for the scarf
- A small amount of superfine green Angora yarn, for the scarf

ITSY BITSY'S BABY
Reduce the templates to 80%.
You will need 2mm (1⁄16in) wire-backed black
glass eyes.

For this project, refer to the templates on page 141.

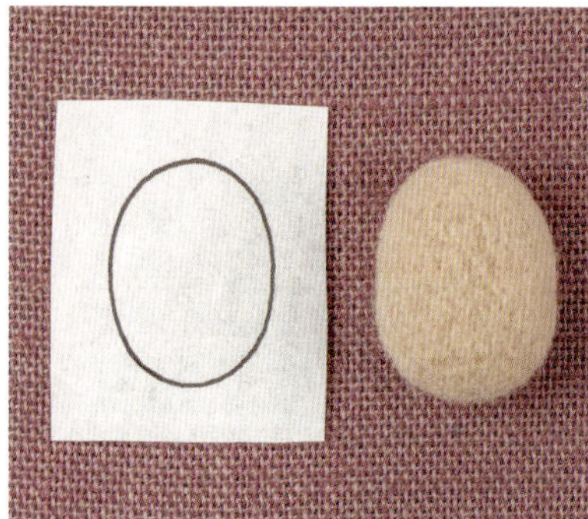

1 Body Following the instructions on page 18 and referring to the template, tightly roll a 6g (¼oz) oval of beige wool and needle felt it until it is firm. Pin-prick the surface with shallow slightly angled stabs to smooth.

2 Head Referring to the template, roll 3g (⅛oz) of wool into a tight sausage and needle felt the end to a point.

3 Needle across 4cm (1½in) of the sausage, before bending the sausage down to create the back of the head. Needle into the back of the bend to secure, leaving loose ends for attaching.

4 Attach the head to the body (see page 21).

5 Referring to the template and using a small amount of wool for each, needle felt the ears, leaving loose fibres (see page 20).

6 Attach the ears.

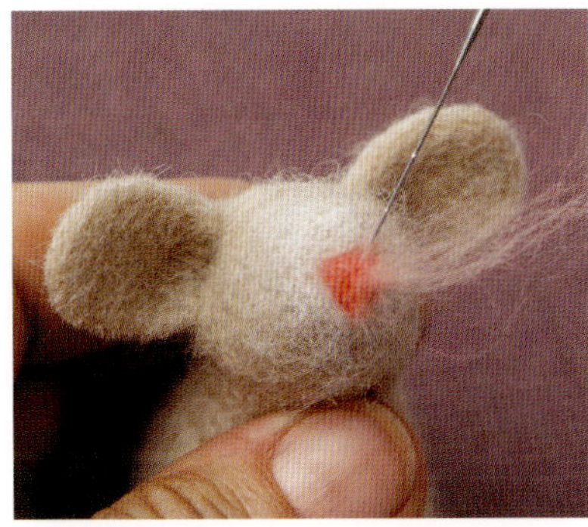

7 Needle a few fibres of white wool into the muzzle. Then, using a thin wisp of pink Merino wool, needle in the pink triangle nose.

8 Using wisps of black Merino wool, needle the vertical nose line and the mouth.

9 Needle repeatedly into the eye areas to create the sockets.

10 Attach the eyes (see page 22).

12 Splay out the fibres, and attach the arms so that one is raised and the other lies flat against the body.

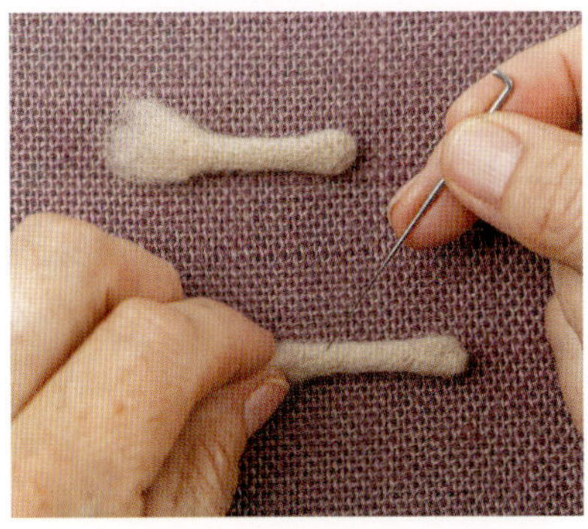

11 Arms Roll a small amount of wool into a tight sausage and needle the end round for the paw. Then needle up the sausage, matching the template, leaving loose fibres. Make two.

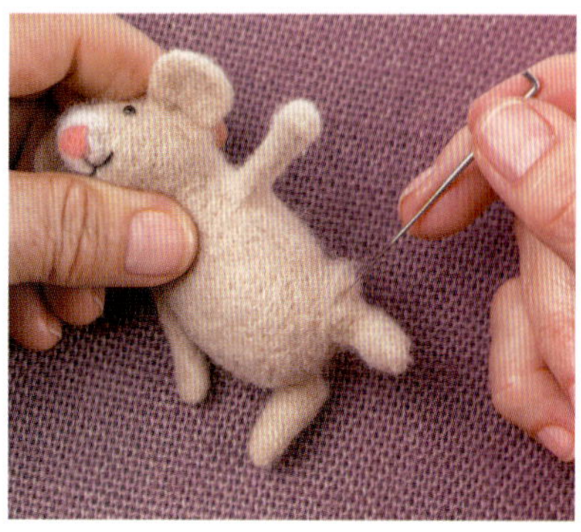

13 Feet Roll a small tight sausage, needle the end round, then work along and around for 3cm (1¼in).

14 Bend the wool to create the heel. Needle into the heel to secure the shape and leave loose fibres for joining. Make two.

15 Attach the feet to the body (see page 21).

16 Needle a little white wool into the chest and on top of the head.

17 Tail Smear a 6cm (2¼in) length of wire with glue, then wrap it with thin lengths of pink Merino wool, leaving 2cm (¾in) unwrapped at one end.

18 Using a bradawl, make a hole in the body for the tail, glue the unwrapped wire end and push it into the hole.

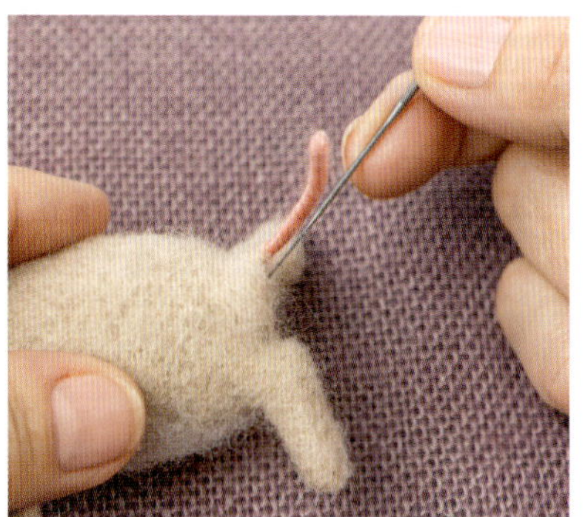

19 To secure the tail, use the 38 triangle needle and wrap beige wool around the wire base, needling firmly into the body.

20 Features Sew three sets of whiskers into the muzzle (see page 23).

21 Lightly brush the cheeks with pink pastel powder.

22 Wrap the raised arm around a mini pine cone and glue it in place.

Knitted Scarf
To keep your mouse warm, knit them a fluffy Angora scarf!

Cast on 7 sts. Knit until the scarf measures 16cm (6¼in).
Cast off.
Sew in the loose ends.
Tie the scarf around Itsy Bitsy's neck.

13

Woolly Alpaca

Alpacas are thought to be the cutest of their ungulate family with their beautiful eyes, long necks and floppy locks. We use Wensleydale locks to emulate their beautiful curly coats.

Finished size

- Alpaca: 14cm (5½in) tall, 11cm (4¼in) long
- Baby: 12.5cm (5in) tall, 8cm (3in) long

What you need

- Templates for size and shape (see page 141)
- Foam pad
- Felting needle: 40 triangle
- Five-needle tool
- Coarse wool: 24g (1oz) white
- Merino wool: a small amount of black
- Wensleydale locks: 5g (¼oz) of small locks, natural
- Two 4mm (³⁄₁₆in) wire-backed glass eyes, black
- Pink pastel powder and a small paintbrush
- Ribbon: 2mm (¹⁄₁₆in) wide by 25cm (10in) long, orange
- Strong clear glue
- Bradawl
- Embroidery scissors

BABY ALPACA
Reduce the templates to 80%.
You will need 3mm (⅛in) wire-backed black
glass eyes and 2mm (1⁄16in) wide by 21cm
(8¼in) long blue ribbon.

For this project, refer to the templates on page 141.

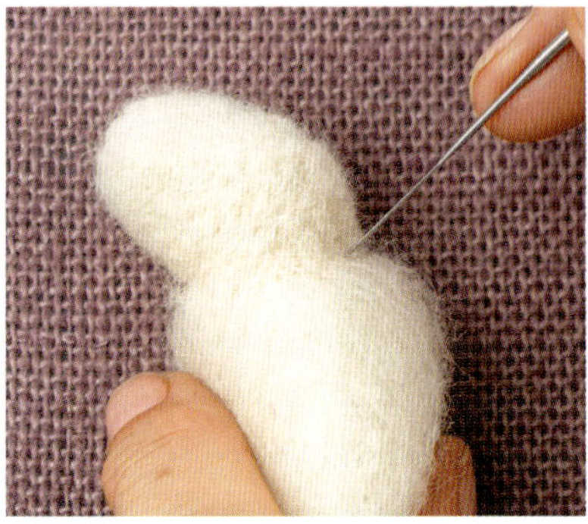

1 Body Following the instructions on page 18, roll 14g (½oz) of wool into a tight oval and needle all over until it is firm and has reduced to the template size.

2 Head and neck Referring to the template, roll 4.5g (¼oz) of wool into a tight sausage and needle felt the end round (see page 18).

3 Bend the wool and needle into the back of the neck.

4 Needle down the sausage to create a long neck. Leave loose fibres for attaching.

5 Splay out the loose fibres and press the bottom of the neck onto the body, so that the alpaca is looking up and slightly to one side. Needle the loose fibres into the body firmly and smoothly.

TIP

As most of the body parts will be covered in curly Wensleydale locks, you will only need to pin-prick the face to smooth the surface. Do this with the needle at a slight angle.

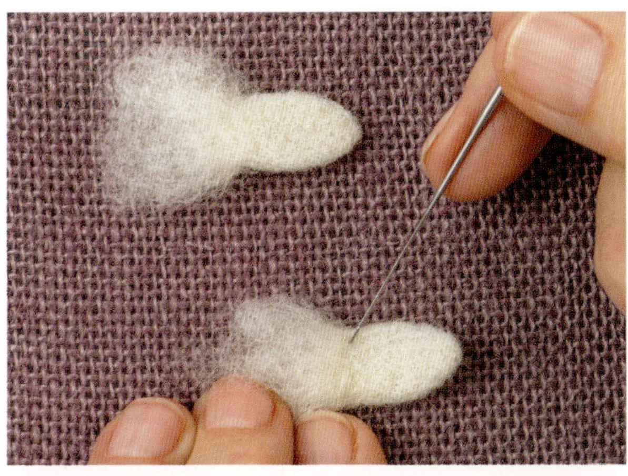

6 Referring to the template and using a small amount of wool for both ears, needle felt them leaving loose fibres.

7 Splay out the loose fibres and attach the ears.

8 Repeatedly needle shallow dips for the eye sockets, and attach the eyes (see page 22).

9 Using wisps of black Merino wool, needle in the nose and mouth lines (see page 22).

10 Legs Referring to the template and using a small amount of wool for each, roll a tight sausage and needle felt one end flat.

11 Needle around and along the sausage, leaving loose fibres for attaching. Make four.

12 Splay out the fibres and press one leg onto the body. Needle in the fibres smoothly and firmly. Repeat for the other three legs.

13 Tail Referring to the template, use a small amount of wool and needle felt a sausage, leaving loose fibres at one end.

14 Splay out the fibres and attach the tail to the body.

15 Lightly brush the nose and cheeks with pink pastel powder.

16 Features Firmly needle lengths of curly Wensleydale locks over the neck, body, legs and tail.

17 Needle more curls around the face and then add extra tufts of Wensleydale locks into the top of the head to create a fluffy topknot.

18 Tie a ribbon bow around the neck and trim the ends.

14

Lovable Lion

With their wild beauty, lions have been an enduring symbol in folklore for tens of thousands of years, often depicting courage and strength. Our wee lions, proud of their heritage, follow this tradition and are looking forward to some big adventures with you.

Finished size

- Lion: 10cm (4in) tall
- Cub: 7cm (2¾in) tall

What you need

- Templates for size and shape (see page 141)
- Foam pad
- Felting needles: 40 triangle, 38 reverse
- Five-needle tool
- Coarse wool: 18g (¾oz) pale yellow, 3g (¼oz) orange, a small amount of white
- Merino wool: a small amount of black
- Two 4mm (³⁄₁₆in) wire-backed glass eyes, black
- White horse hair for whiskers
- Orange yarn: 15cm (6in)
- Large eye needle
- Autofade pen
- Strong clear glue
- Bradawl
- Embroidery scissors
- Crown: 15mm (½in) diameter, gold

LION CUB

Reduce the template to 80%. You will
need 3mm (⅛in) wire-backed black glass
eyes. Instead of a mane, needle a few
orange fibres into the head.

For this project, refer to the templates on page 141.

1 Body Following the instructions on pages 16–17 and referring to the template, roll 6g (¼oz) of yellow wool into a tight ball. Needle evenly and deeply all over until it is firm and matches the template.

2 Head Roll 4g (⅛oz) of wool into a tight ball. Needle evenly and deeply all over until firm and matches the template. Leave loose fibres for attaching.

3 Splay out the loose fibres, and pressing the head onto the body at a slight angle, needle them into the body firmly and smoothly (see page 21).

4 For the nose, referring to the template and using a small amount of yellow wool, needle felt the shape.

5 Turn it over and needle the back flat, leaving loose fibres at the top and bottom of the nose for attaching.

6 To attach the nose, splay out the loose fibres, and needle them into the head smoothly and firmly. Needle around the edge of the sides and the bottom, to secure.

7 Repeatedly needle to create shallow dips for the eye sockets, and attach the eyes (see page 22).

8 Using thin lengths of black Merino wool, gently needle in the nose.

9 Needle three small soft white balls and attach them under the nose.

10 Using thin wisps of black Merino wool, needle in the vertical line, and then the mouth.

11 Referring to the template and using a small amount of wool for each, needle felt the ears leaving loose fibres (see page 20).

12 Splay out the loose fibres and attach the ears (see page 21).

13 Legs Roll a tight sausage using 2g (¹⁄₁₆oz) of wool. Needle the end flat.

14 Needle up and around the sausage until it matches the template, leaving loose fibres for attaching. Make two.

15 Splay out the loose fibres. Press the leg onto the body and attach both, making sure that your lion is sitting correctly.

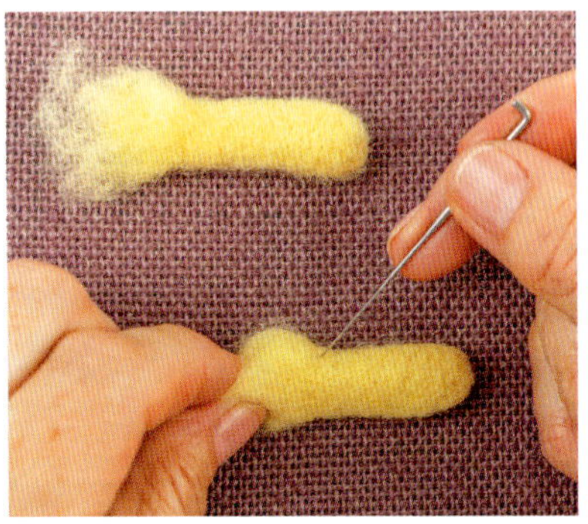

16 Arms Roll two tight sausages using a small amount of wool for each. Needle the bottom ends round. Now needle the sausages to match the template. Leave loose fibres for attaching.

17 Attach one arm so that it curves towards the body.

18 Attach the other arm so it is waving, needling the loose ends into the body smoothly and firmly.

19 Mane Draw the outline with an autofade pen.

20 Fill the area with approximately 3g (¹⁄₈oz) orange wool, adding more fibres to build up a smooth, rounded shape.

21 Work over the mane with a reverse needle for a fluffy finish.

22 Trim to neaten, then crown your lion.

23 Tail Needle a small tuft of orange wool onto a length of orange yarn.

24 Sew it on so that it measures 3.5cm (1¼in).

25 Sew whiskers into the face (see page 23).

15

Cassandra Panda

Cassandra and her cub are really good swimmers and climbers! They live in a bamboo forest where tasty leaves, stems and shoots are their absolute favourite treats (although they would never say 'no' to a drop of honey). We hope you love these cute animals as much as we do.

Finished size

- Cassandra: 9cm (3½in) tall
- Cub: 7.5cm (3in) tall

What you need

- Templates for size and shape (see page 141)
- Foam pad
- Felting needles: 40 triangle, 38 reverse
- Five-needle tool
- Coarse wool: 11g (⅜oz) white, 9g (¼oz) black
- Merino wool: a small amount of black
- Two 4mm (³⁄₁₆in) wire-backed glass eyes, black
- Autofade pen
- Strong clear glue
- Bradawl
- Embroidery scissors

CASSANDRA'S CUB
Reduce the templates to 80%. You will need 3mm (⅛in) black glass eyes. When complete, work over the body and the top of the head with a reverse needle to create a fluffy look.

1 Body Following the instructions on pages 16–17, roll 6g (¼oz) of white wool into a tight ball. Needle evenly and deeply all over, into a rounded triangle shape, until it becomes firm and matches the template.

2 Head Referring to the template, roll 4g (⅛oz) of white wool into a tight ball. Needle all over until it is firm and matches the template. Leave loose fibres to attach to the body.

3 Splay out the loose neck fibres, press the head onto the body (just slightly to one side, to create a tilt), then needle the loose ends in smoothly and firmly.

4 Referring to the template and using a small amount of black wool for each, needle felt the ears leaving loose fibres (see page 20).

5 Splay out the fibres and attach the ears.

TIP

To cover any trailing black fibres at the base of the ear, needle a few white fibres over them and pin-prick them smooth.

6 For the muzzle, use a small amount of white wool and roll a tight cone shape. Needle all round, leaving loose fibres for attaching (see page 19).

7 Splay out the loose fibres, press the muzzle onto the head and needle the fibres in smoothly and firmly.

8 Using thin lengths of black Merino wool, needle the nose, then add the vertical nose line and mouth (see page 22).

9 Needle a small soft ball for the bottom lip and attach it just below the mouth line.

10 Using an autofade pen, draw in the eye patch outlines.

11 Fill in with coarse wool, covering the two areas completely.

12 Attach the eyes (see page 22).

13 Needle approximately 2g (¹⁄₁₆oz) of black wool into the upper half of the body.

14 Legs Referring to the template and using 2g (¹⁄₁₆oz) of wool for each, roll two tight sausages and needle the ends flat. Needle up and around the sausages until firm leaving loose fibres.

15 Splay out the loose fibres and attach the legs so that your panda is in a firm sitting position.

16 Arms Referring to the template and using a small amount of wool for each, roll two tight sausages. Needle one end round, then needle up and around the sausages until they are firm, leaving loose fibres for attaching.

17 Splay out the fibres and attach the arms. Attach one of them so that the panda is waving.

18 Tail Needle felt a small cone (see page 19), leaving loose fibres at one end. Attach it smoothly and firmly.

19 Use the reverse needle to pull fibres out of the top of the head to create a fluffy finish.

20 Use the reverse needle to pull fibres out of the lower body, to create a fluffy finish. Trim back any long fibres on the head and body to neaten.

16

Roly Polar Bear

Our polar bears, with their super paws, are perfectly adapted for swimming
– which they love! In the Arctic wild their big feet help them walk on the ice
too. Capturing their cuteness is simple: features can be adjusted to achieve
the look you want, and tilting a head will add to the appeal.

Finished size

- Roly: 10.5cm (4in) tall, 12cm (4¾in) long
- Cub: 8cm (3in) tall, 9.5cm (3¾in) long

What you need

- Templates for size and shape (see page 142)
- Foam pad
- Felting needles: 40 triangle, 38 reverse
- Five-needle tool
- Coarse wool: 30g (1oz) white
- Merino wool: a small amount of black
- Two 3mm (⅛in) wire-backed glass eyes, black
- Pink pastel powder and a small paintbrush
- Strong clear glue
- Bradawl
- Embroidery scissors

ROLY'S CUB
Reduce the templates to 80%. You will need 2mm (1⁄16in) wire-backed black glass eyes. Tilt the muzzle up slightly.

For this project, refer to the templates on page 142.

1 Body Following the instructions on page 18, roll 14g (½oz) of white wool into a tight oval and needle all over until it is firm and has reduced to the template size.

2 Head Lay 4.5g (⅛oz) of wool on the pad and fold the fibres on the right into the centre.

3 Referring to the template, roll the wool into a tight sausage and needle one end round for the nose.

4 Needle along and around the sausage, leaving loose fibres at the other end for attaching.

5 Splay out the fibres, press the head onto the body at a slight angle, then needle the loose ends into the body firmly and smoothly (see page 21). Add more wool if needed to create a smooth body contour.

6 Referring to the template, use 2g (¹⁄₁₆oz) of wool to needle felt the muzzle, then attach it.

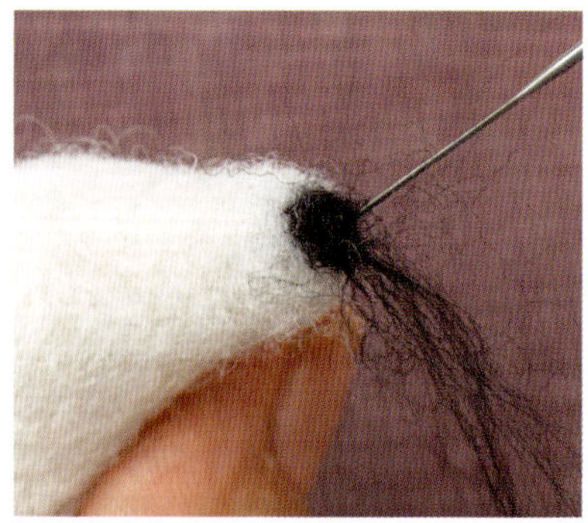

7 Using thin wisps of black Merino wool, needle in the nose.

8 Add the smile line.

9 Repeatedly needle to create shallow dips for the eye sockets, and attach the eyes (see page 22).

10 Referring to the template and using a small amount of wool for each, needle felt the ears, leaving loose fibres (see page 20).

11 Attach the ears.

12 Legs Referring to the template and using 2.5g (⅛oz) of wool for each, roll a tight sausage and needle the end flat.

13 Needle along and around the sausage until it matches the template and is firm, leaving loose fibres. Make four.

14 Splay out the fibres and press one leg onto the body. Needle the loose ends in smoothly and firmly. Repeat for the other three legs.

15 Tail Needle felt a small sausage, leaving loose fibres at one end. Attach it firmly and smoothly to the body.

16 Lightly brush the cheeks with pink pastel powder.

17 To create a fluffy look, pull the fibres out of the top of the head, body and legs using the reverse needle, then trim any big tufts to neaten.

17

Dinky Donkey

Donkeys are sensitive, gentle and loyal, and never happier than when they are loved and cherished. Our little donkeys are looking for a warm home where they can share the joys of creativity and friendship. Remember – always refer to the template and start off each shape by rolling the wool tightly. Enjoy the felting process and have fun.

Finished size

- Dinky: 16cm (6¼in) tall, 12cm (4¾in) long
- Foal: 11cm (4¼in) tall, 7cm (2¾in) long

What you need

- Templates for size and shape (see page 142)
- Foam pad
- Felting needle: 40 triangle
- Five-needle tool
- Coarse wool: approximately 28g (1oz) grey, 2g (1⁄16oz) white, a small amount of black
- Merino wool: a small amount of black
- Yarn: a 15cm (6in) length of grey for the tail
- Two 5mm (¼in) wire-backed glass eyes, black
- Sewing needle
- Strong clear glue
- Bradawl
- Embroidery scissors

DINKY'S FOAL
Reduce the templates to 80%.
You will need 3mm (⅛in) wire-backed
black glass eyes.

For this project, refer to the templates on page 142.

1 Body Following the instructions on page 18, roll 14g (½oz) of grey wool into a tight oval and needle all over until it is firm and has reduced to the template size. Pin-prick all over at a slight angle until smooth.

2 Head and neck Roll 6g (¼oz) of grey wool into a tight sausage and needle the end round for the nose.

3 Needle the sausage all around until it measures 3cm (1¼in), then bend it down to create the neck.

4 Needle into the bend to secure. Then needle the rest of the sausage so that the neck gradually thickens, until it matches the template. Leave loose fibres for attaching.

5 Splay out the loose fibres, press the neck onto the body with the head turned slightly, then needle the fibres into the body firmly and smoothly (see page 21).

6 Referring to the template and using a small amount of wool for each, needle felt the ears leaving loose fibres (see page 20).

7 Needle a few white fibres into the lower half of each one.

8 Splay out the loose fibres and attach the ears.

9 Repeatedly needle to create shallow dips for the eye sockets, and attach the eyes (see page 22).

10 Needle a small amount of white wool above each eye.

11 Outline the muzzle with white wool.

12 Needle white wool into the muzzle.

13 Using a thin wisp of black Merino wool, needle the smile line.

14 Legs Referring to the template and using a small amount of grey wool for each, needle felt four legs, leaving loose fibres where indicated.

TIP

For a neater finish, more wool can be needled into the top of the legs to fill in any dips and hollows.

15 Splay out the fibres, press each leg onto the body, then needle the loose ends in firmly and smoothly. Make sure that your donkey can stand, adjusting if needed.

16 Needle white wool into the underside of the body and up into the chest.

17 Needle some black wool into the top of the head and down the neck for the mane.

18 Needle a cross onto your donkey's back using thin wisps of black wool. Trim the mane fibres back to approximately 5mm (¼in).

19 Tail Needle some black wool onto the end of a 15cm (6in) length of grey yarn.

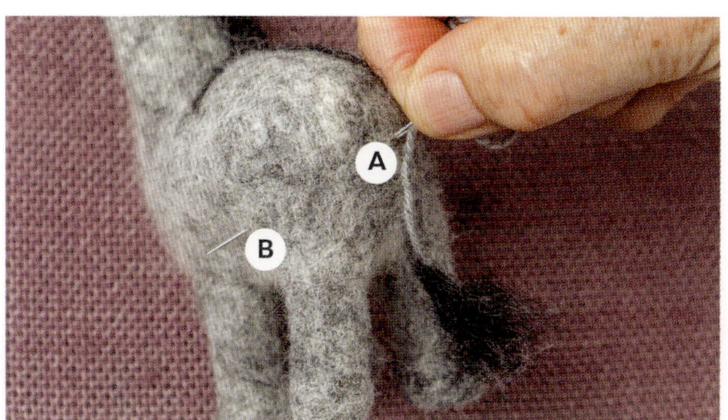

20 To attach the tail, thread the yarn through the body at point A, pulling your needle out at point B.

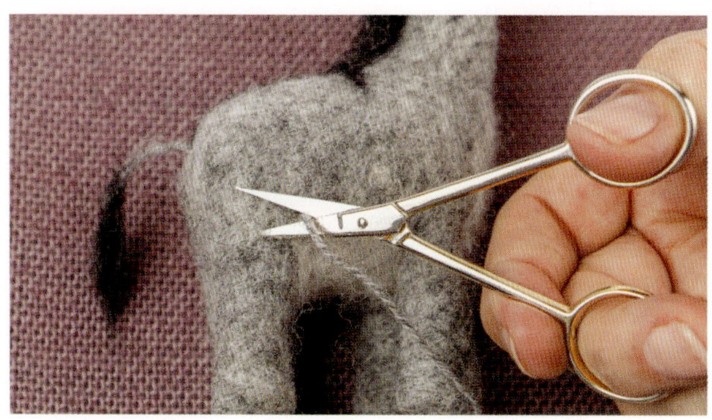

21 Thread the yarn back through the body and trim. The tail should be 3.5cm (1¼in) long.

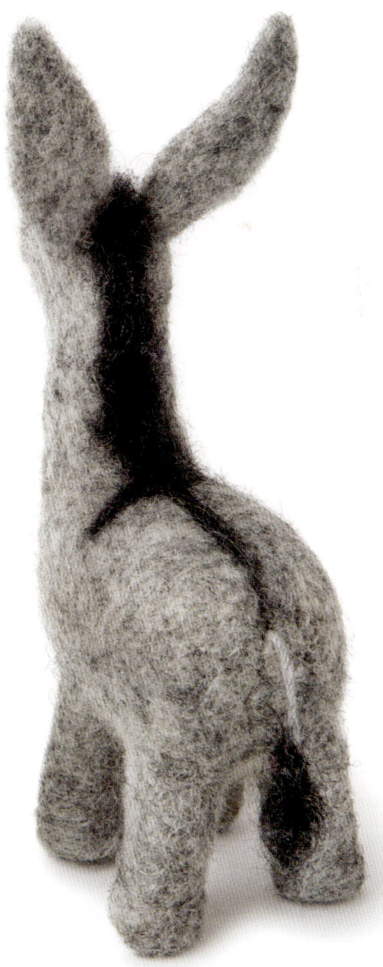

18

Ellie Elephant

We just had to include elephants, loving their tender hearts and strong family bonds. In their wild world they form tight-knit groups, the herds usually being ruled by a matriarch. With her experience and strength she ensures the wellbeing and survival of every member, bringing protection to all and a wealth of crucial knowledge. Our own little mother elephant and her calf are looking for a new life and a place to call home.
So, enjoy making them and have fun.

Finished size

- Ellie: 10cm (4in) tall, 14cm (5½in) long
- Calf: 8cm (3in) tall, 8cm (3in) long

What you need

- Templates for size and shape (see page 142)
- Foam pad
- Felting needle: 40 triangle
- Five-needle tool
- Coarse wool: approximately 33g (1¼oz) grey
- Merino wool: a small amount of black
- Yarn: a 20cm (8in) length of grey for the tail
- Two 4mm (³⁄₁₆in) wire-backed glass eyes, black
- Red pastel powder and a small paintbrush
- Sewing needle
- Strong clear glue
- Bradawl
- Embroidery scissors
- Small fabric flower

ELLIE'S CALF
Reduce the templates to 80%.
You will need 3mm (⅛in)
wire-backed black glass eyes.

1 Body Following the instructions on page 18, roll 14g (½oz) of grey wool into a tight oval one third larger than the template and needle all over until it is firm and has reduced to the template size. Then pin-prick the surface to smooth.

2 Head and trunk Referring to the template, roll 6g (¼oz) of wool into a tight sausage so it is thinner at one end. Needle this end flat for the end of the trunk.

3 Work up the trunk needling the fibres and gradually thickening and shaping them. Leave loose ends for attaching.

4 Needle a slight bend towards the end of the trunk, to create a slight curve upwards.

5 To attach the head, splay out the loose fibres and press them onto the body, then needle the loose fibres in firmly and smoothly (see page 21).

6 Referring to the template and using a small amount of wool for each, needle felt the ears leaving loose fibres (see page 20).

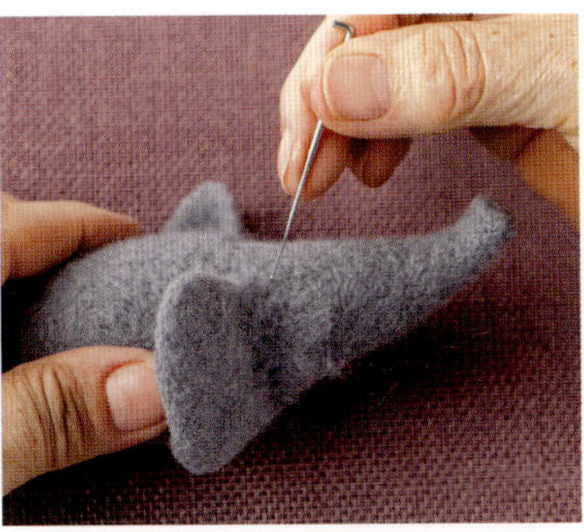

7 Splay out the loose fibres and attach the ears.

8 Needle felt a bottom lip, then attach it at the base of the trunk.

9 Repeatedly needle a smile line either side of the lip to create an indent.

10 Legs Referring to the template, roll a tight sausage using 2g (¹⁄₁₆oz) of wool. Needle one end flat for the foot.

11 Then needle up and around the sausage until it is firm, leaving loose fibres at the top. Make two – these are the front legs.

12 In the same way, using 2.5g (⅛oz) of wool, needle felt two slightly shorter back legs. Splay out the loose fibres, press each leg onto the body and needle the loose ends in firmly and smoothly, making sure that your elephant can stand.

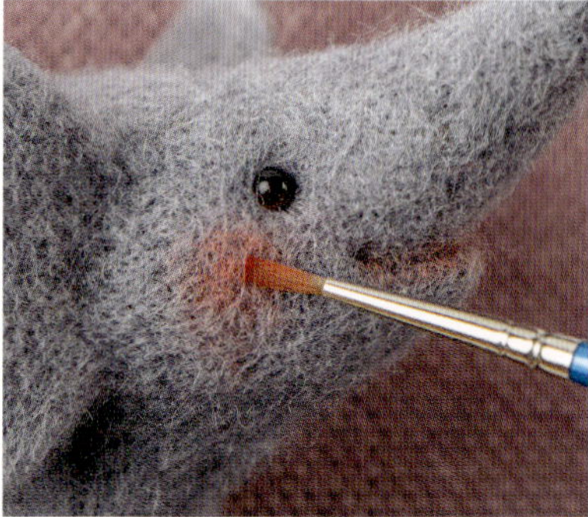

13 Eyes Repeatedly needle the two areas on either side of the trunk to create shallow dips for the eye sockets.

14 Attach the eyes (see page 22).

15 Lightly brush the lips and cheeks with a little red pastel powder to give a soft blush.

16 Features Needle a wisp of black Merino wool into a smile line.

17 Needle a tuft of grey wool onto the top of the head and trim across to neaten.

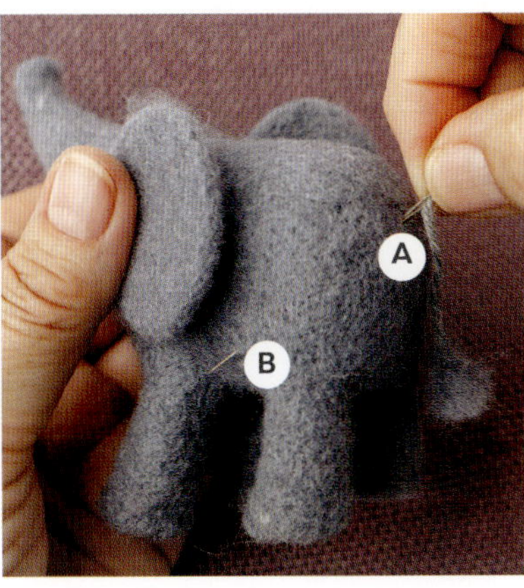

18 Tail Needle a little grey wool onto the end of a 15cm (6in) length of grey yarn.

19 To attach the tail, thread the yarn through the body at point A, pulling your needle out at point B.

20 Thread the yarn back through the body and trim the ends. The tail coming out of the body should be approximately 3.5cm (1¼in) in length.

21 Glue a small fabric flower to the end of the trunk.

Gillian Giraffe

The tallest animals in the world, these gentle giants have unique markings, just like our fingerprints. They spend most of their time eating, their long necks allowing them to reach the leaves and buds way up high in the treetops. Most of all they love the flowers, fruit and leaves of the acacia tree. Giraffes can run extremely fast too, so make sure when you are making Gillian and her calf that their legs are firmly attached!

Finished size

- Gillian: 17cm (6½in) tall, 13cm (5in) long
- Calf: 12cm (4¾in) tall, 9cm (3½in) long

What you need

- Templates for size and shape (see page 143)
- Foam pad
- Felting needle: 40 triangle
- Five-needle tool
- Coarse wool: approximately 34g (1¼oz) off-white, 5g (¼oz) orange
- Merino wool: a small amount of black
- Yarn: 15cm (6in) length of orange for the tail
- Two 6mm (¼in) wire-backed glass eyes, black
- Orange pastel powder and a medium paintbrush
- Sewing needle
- Strong clear glue
- Bradawl
- Embroidery scissors

GILLIAN'S CALF
Reduce the templates to 80%.
You will need 4mm (³⁄₁₆in) wire-backed
black glass eyes. To finish, needle a
small tuft of orange wool into the top of
the head.

For this project, refer to the templates on page 143.

1 Body Following the instructions on page 18, roll 14g (½oz) of white wool into a tight oval one third larger than the template. Needle all over until it is firm and has reduced to the template size.

2 Head and neck Referring to the template, roll 7g (¼oz) of wool into a tight sausage and needle one end round for the nose.

3 Needle the sausage until it measures 4cm (1½in), then bend the shape down to create the neck.

4 Needle into the bend to secure, then needle all around and along the rest of the sausage until it matches the template. Leave loose fibres for attaching.

5 Splay out the loose fibres, press the neck onto the body, then needle the loose ends in firmly and smoothly. If necessary, add more wool around the join to neaten.

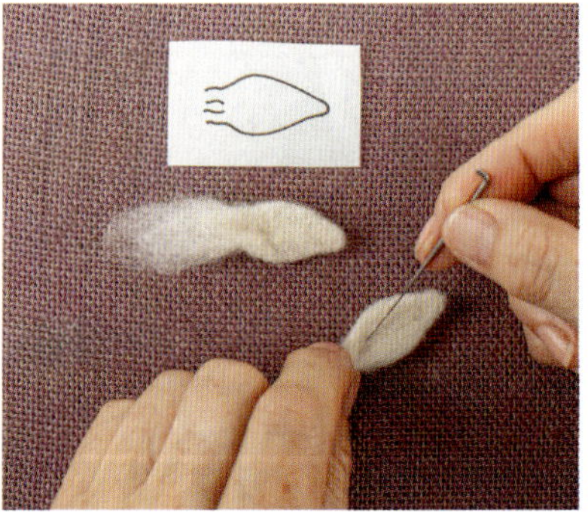

6 Referring to the template and using a small amount of wool for each, needle felt the ears leaving loose fibres (see page 20).

7 Splay out the loose fibres and attach the ears.

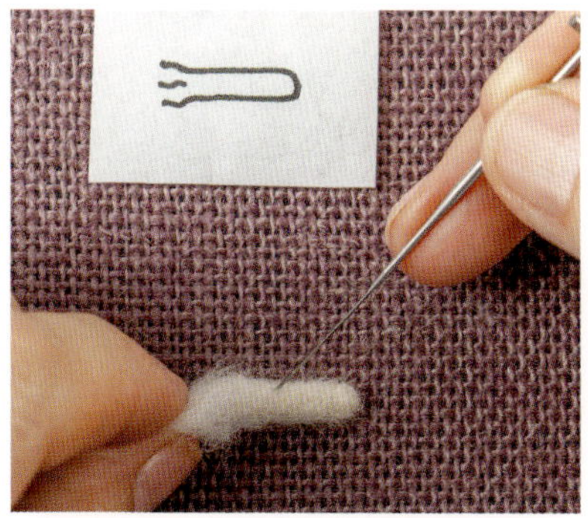 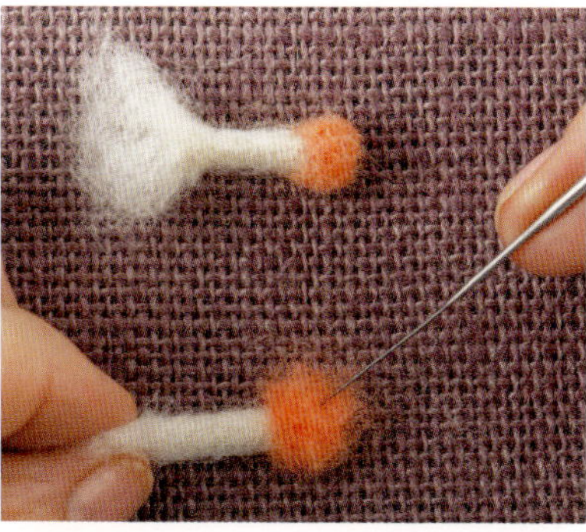 

8 Roll a small amount of white wool into a tight sausage and needle the fibres until they match the horn template. Make two.

9 Wrap a little orange wool around the end of one and needle it into a small ball. Repeat.

10 Attach the horns.

11 Using a pulled length of orange wool, outline the muzzle area.

12 Fill in the area with more orange wool and needle until smooth and rounded.

13 Using a wisp of Merino wool, needle the smile line.

14 Attach the eyes (see page 22).

15 Needle a tuft of wool to the top of the head. Trim across to neaten.

16 Legs Roll a tight sausage using 2.5g (⅛oz) of wool and needle the end flat.

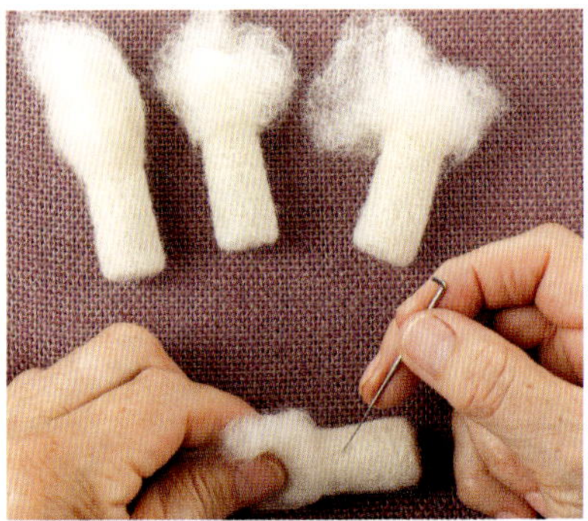

17 Referring to the template, needle up and around the sausage until firm, leaving loose fibres at the top. Make four.

18 Splay out the fibres, press each leg onto the body and needle the loose ends in firmly and smoothly making sure that your giraffe can stand.

19 Markings Brush a line of orange pastel powder between the eyes.

20 Brush more powder down the neck and along the top of the body.

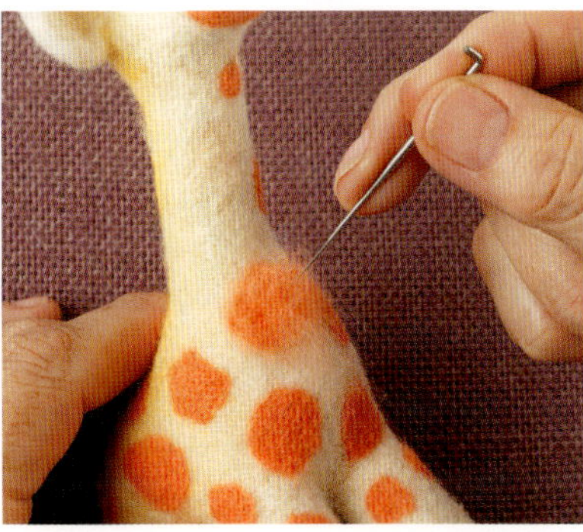

21 Using 3g (⅛oz) of wool, needle patches of orange wool over the legs, body and neck.

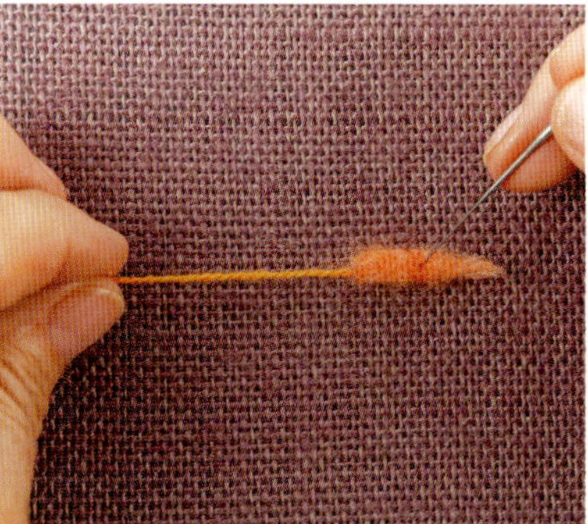

22 Tail Needle a small amount of orange wool into a teardrop shape, and needle this onto the end of a length of orange yarn.

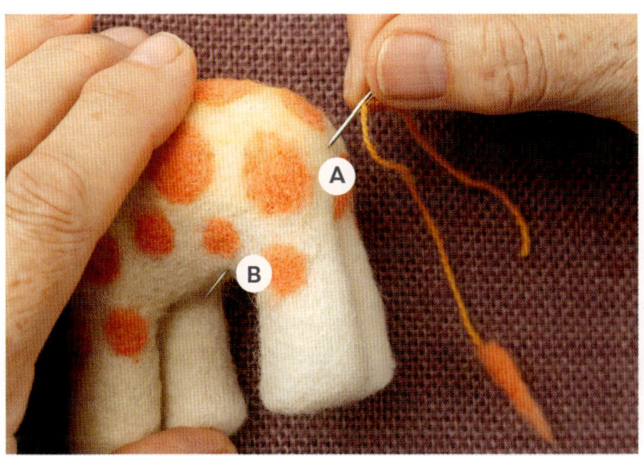

23 Thread the other end onto a needle and push it through the body at point A, pulling your needle out at point B.

24 Push the needle back through your giraffe to secure.

25 Trim the loose end. The yarn tail should be 3.5cm (1¼in) long.

20

Cuddly Kangaroo

Kangaroos live in groups and communicate with nose touching, thumping their hind legs on the ground and protective growling. They are the only large animals that hop, and clear impressive heights with just one jump. Their joeys are tiny when born. A joey stays in its mother's pouch for six months before making small trips outside. Our little joey is happy to be part of our woolly group, and this family is looking forward to meeting you.

Finished size

- Kangaroo: 16cm (6¼in) tall
- Joey: 12cm (4¾in) tall
- Pouch Joey: 6cm (2¼)

What you need

- Templates for size and shape (see page 143)
- Foam pad
- Felting needle: 40 triangle
- Five-needle tool
- Coarse wool: approximately 35g (1¼oz) beige, a small amount of white
- Merino wool: a small amount of black
- Two 4mm (³⁄₁₆in) wire-backed glass eyes, black
- Brown pastel powder and a small paintbrush
- Strong clear glue
- Bradawl
- Embroidery scissors

JOEYS
For the standing joey, reduce the
templates to 80%. To make the pouch
joey, reduce just the kangaroo head and ear
templates by 50%. You will need 2mm (¹⁄₁₆in)
wire-backed black glass eyes for each joey.

For this project, refer to the templates on page 143.

1 Body Following the instructions on page 18, roll 14g (½oz) of beige wool into a tight oval and needle felt it until it is firm and matches the template.

2 Head Referring to the template, roll 4g (⅛oz) of beige wool into a tight sausage. Needle felt one end into a slightly pointed shape for the nose.

3 Needle up and around the shape, gradually thickening it as you work, and using the template as your guide. Then bend the wool downwards, to create the neck, and needle into the bend.

4 Referring to the template, work down the neck. Then splay out the loose fibres, press the head onto the body and needle the loose ends in firmly to secure.

5 Referring to the template and using a small amount of wool for each, needle felt the ears leaving loose fibres (see page 20).

6 Splay out the loose fibres and attach the ears.

7 Attach the eyes (see page 22).

8 Using thin wisps of black Merino wool, needle in the nose (see page 22).

9 Needle in a few white fibres beneath the nose, then needle in the black vertical line and smile line.

10 For the bottom lip, needle felt and attach a small ball of white wool beneath the smile line.

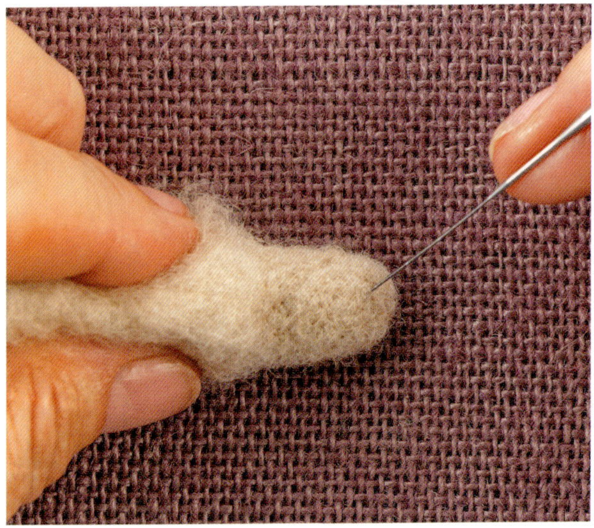

11 Legs Using 2.5g (¹⁄₁₆oz) of wool, roll a tight sausage then needle one end round to match the template.

12 Needle along and around the sausage until it measures 3.5cm (1½in), bend the foot, then needle into the bend firmly to secure the fibres and create the heel. Needle into the bottom of the foot to flatten it.

13 Referring to the template, needle felt the haunch so that it is rounded, leaving loose fibres for attaching. Make two.

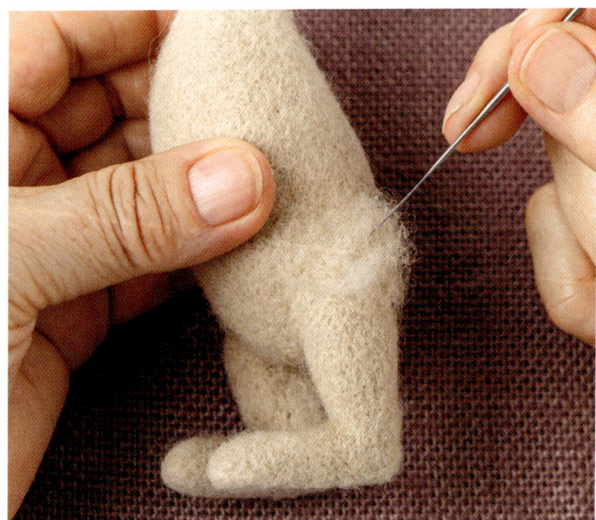

14 Splay out the fibres and attach the legs, making sure that your kangaroo is standing upright.

15 Tail Referring to the template, roll 4g (⅛oz) of wool into a tight sausage so it is thinner at one end, then needle this end round.

16 Turn the tail, and gradually work along and around the shape, thickening it by packing (poking) the wool into the pointed end to firm it up. Bend the tail towards the thicker end to match the template, leaving loose ends for attaching.

17 Splay out the fibres, press the tail onto the body so that your kangaroo has a secure standing pose, then needle the loose fibres into the body smoothly and firmly.

18 Arms Referring to the template, needle felt the two 'sausage' arms, leaving loose fibres for attaching.

19 Attach the arms.

20 Gently brush brown pastel powder onto the paws, inner ears and around the eyes.

21 Pouch Lay a 2g (¹⁄₁₆oz) 7 x 6cm (2¾ x 2⅓in) rectangle of wool on the pad and needle the surface to start the felting process.

22 Flip the shape repeatedly and use the five-needle tool so that it becomes firm and felted.

23 Fold the top over and needle along the fold to neaten. Use the five-needle tool again and continue felting until it is firm.

24 Lay the pouch on the kangaroo's tummy, making sure to create a gap for the baby joey, then needle the loose fibres in smoothly and firmly.

25 Baby joey Use 3g (⅛oz) of wool, and reduce the template by 50% to make the baby joey's head and ears.

26 Add a little extra wool to the neck, then needle to create a soft rounded body.

27 Push the baby's body into the pouch.

Templates

The templates are all reproduced at actual size.

Katie Koala – page 26

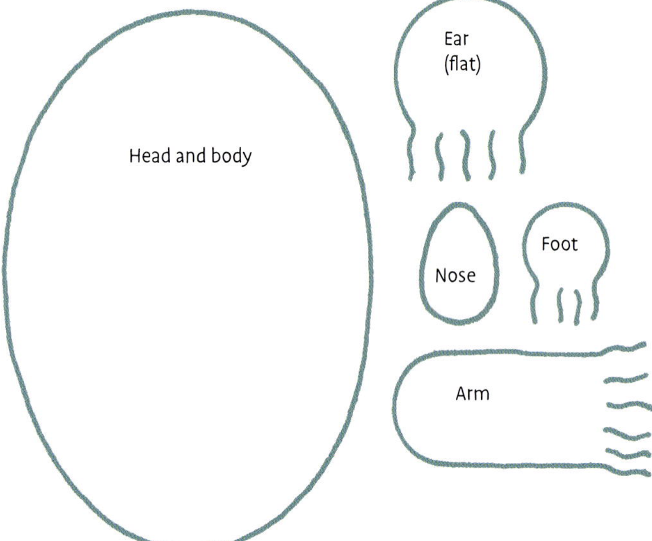

Hootie Owl – page 36

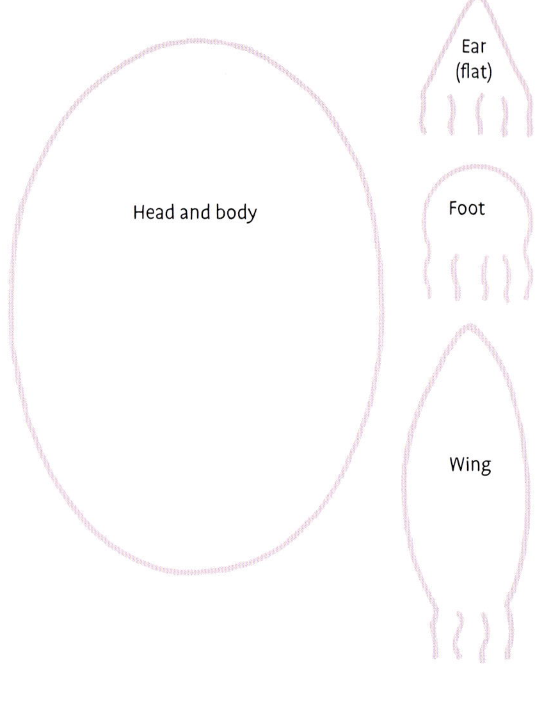

Pippin Penguin – page 30

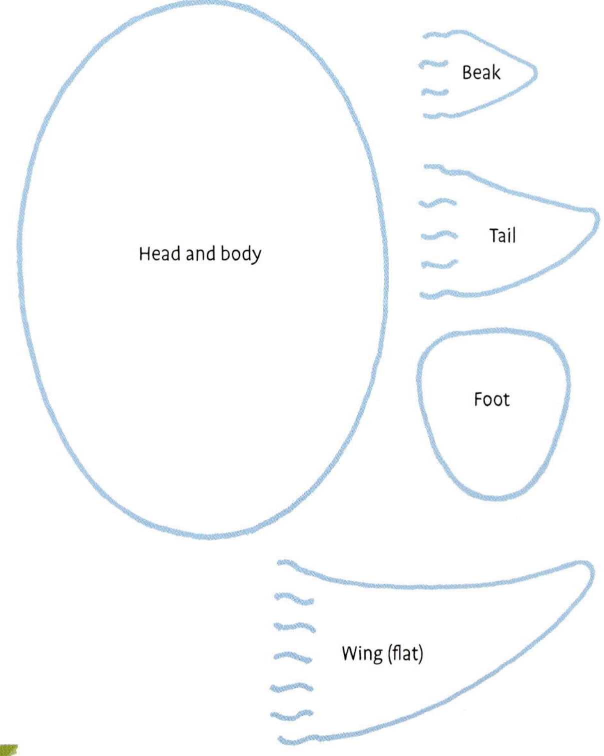

Bonny Bunny – page 40

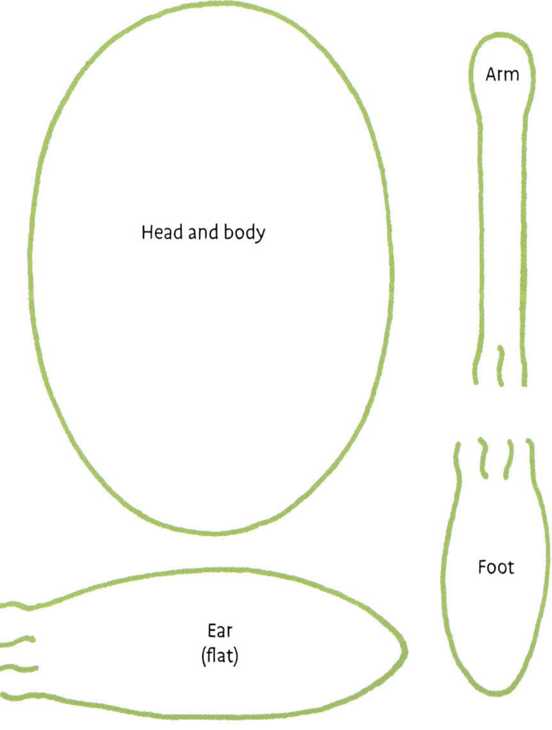

Fabulous Fox – page 46

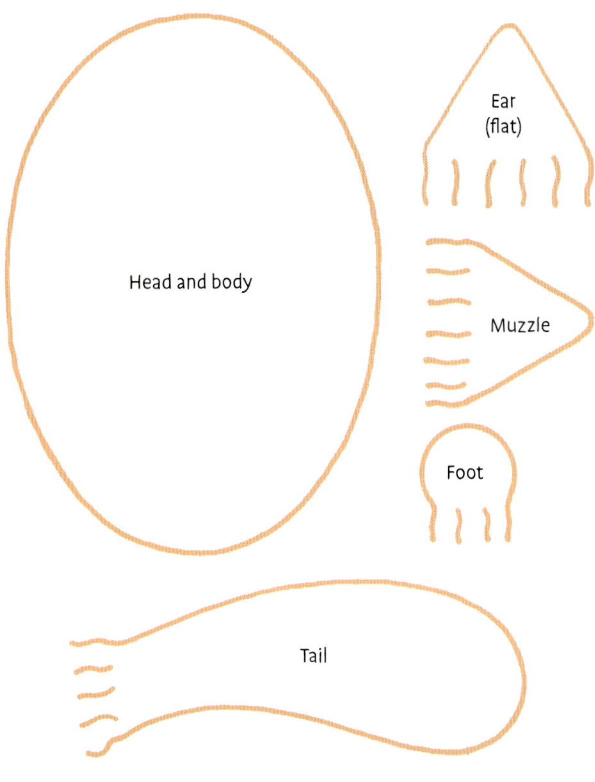

Timmy Guinea Pig – page 52

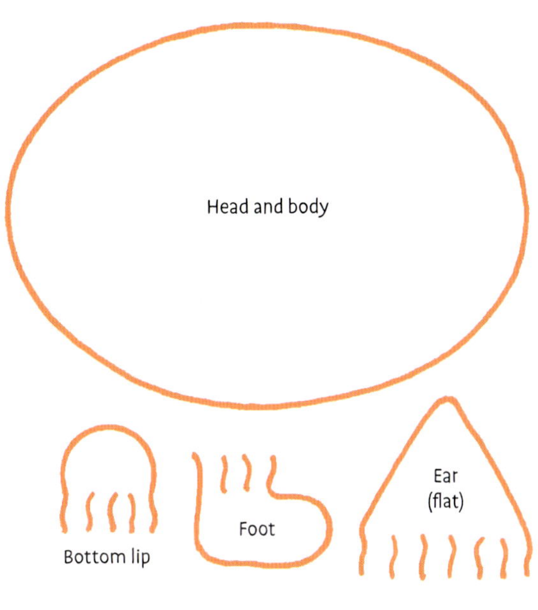

Happy Hedgehog – page 58

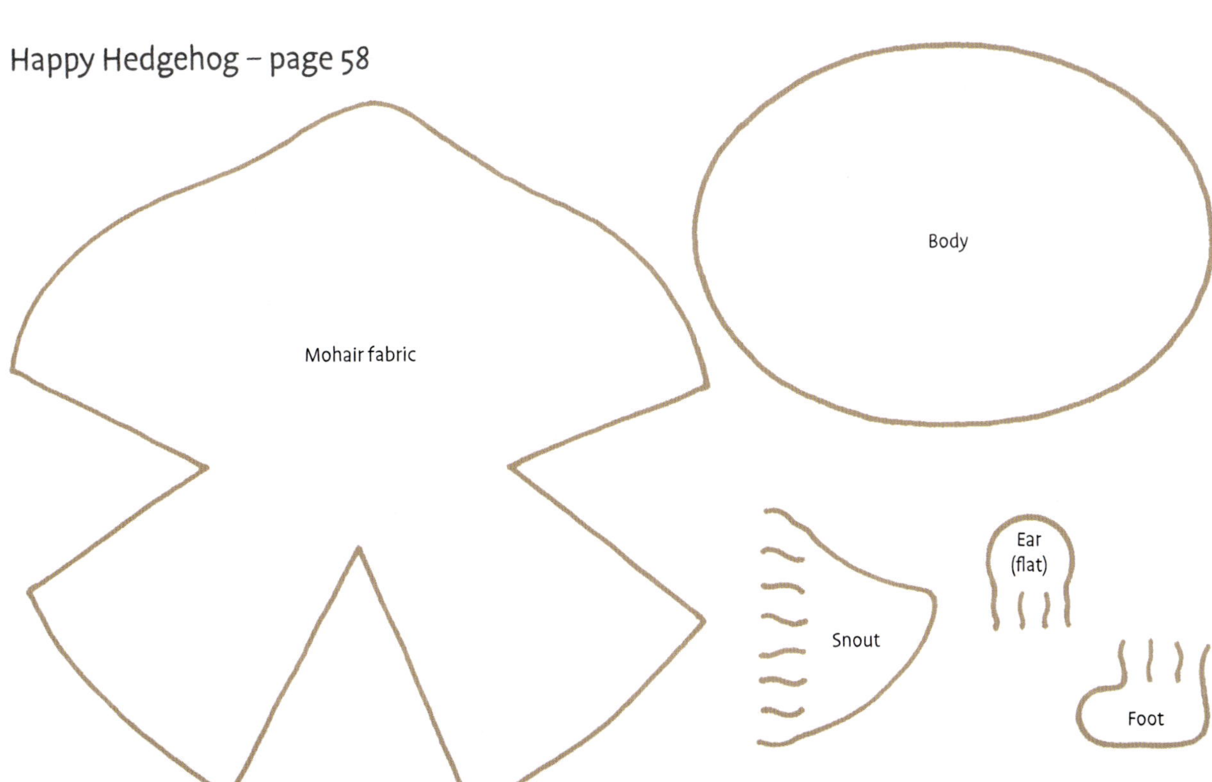

Eliza Hen – page 64

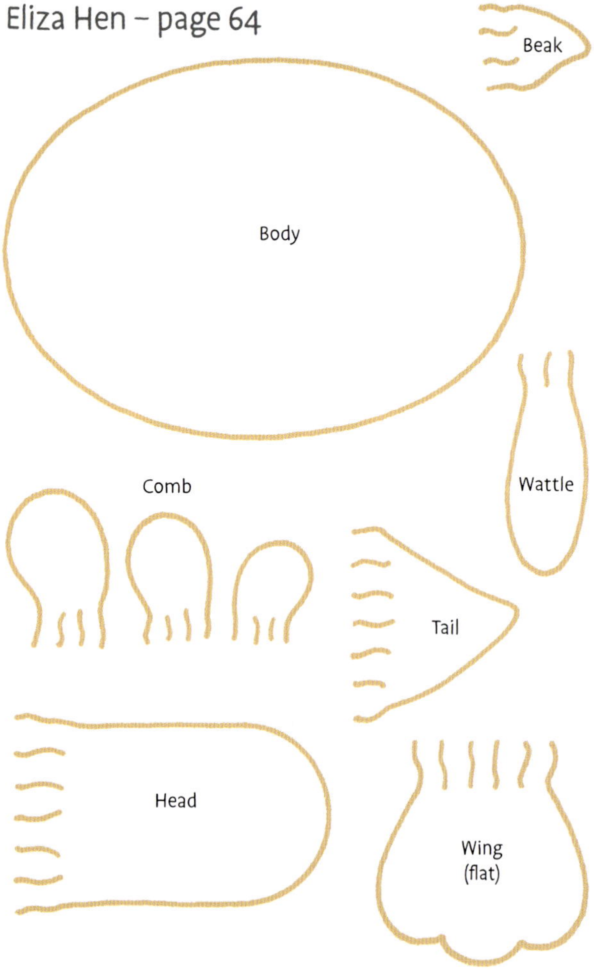

Snuggly Sheep – page 70

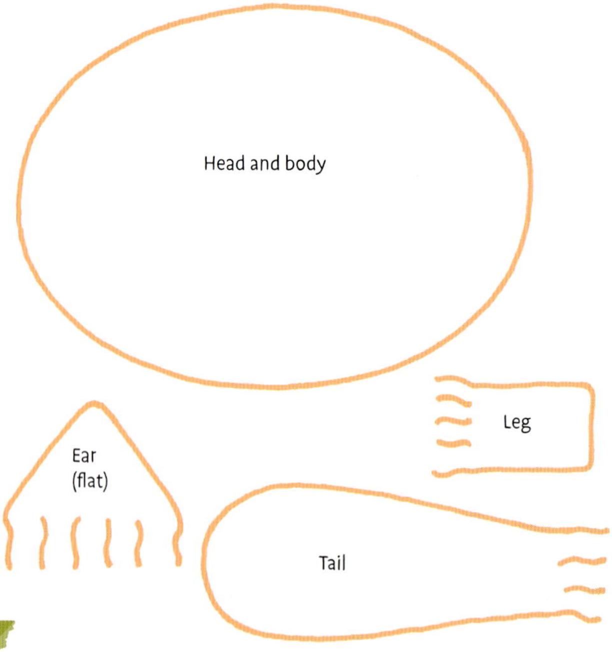

Waggy Dog – page 78

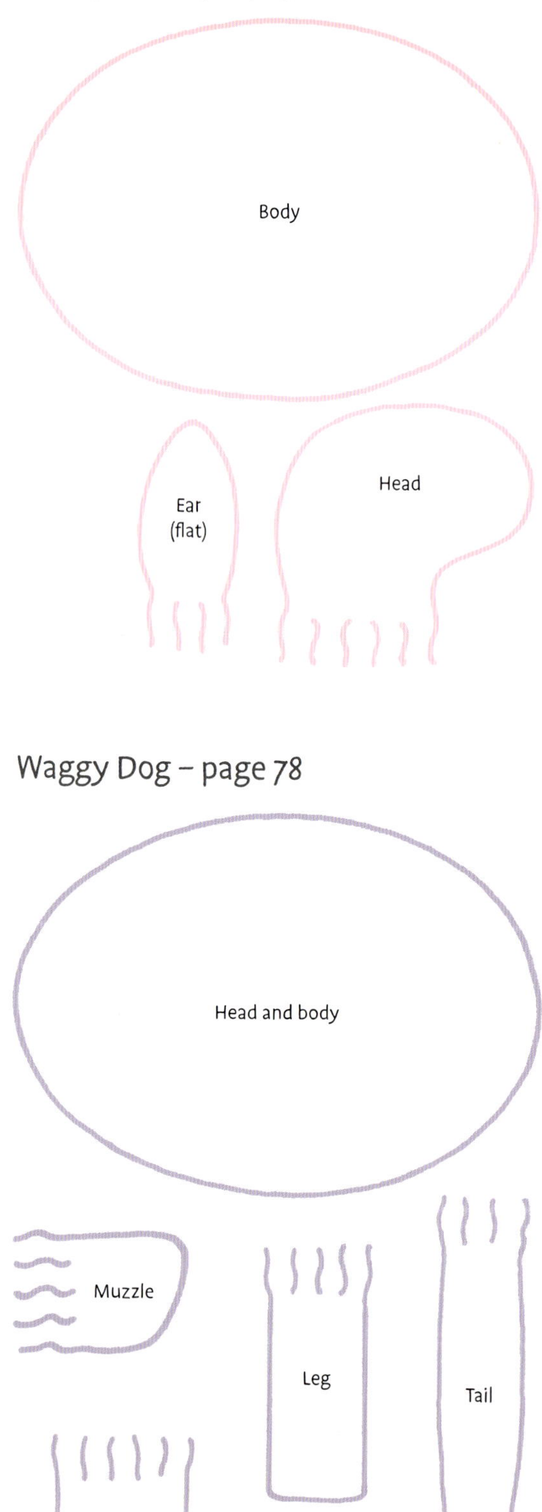

Cozy Cat – page 74

Itsy Bitsy Mouse – page 84

Woolly Alpaca – page 90

Lovable Lion – page 96

Cassandra Panda – page 102

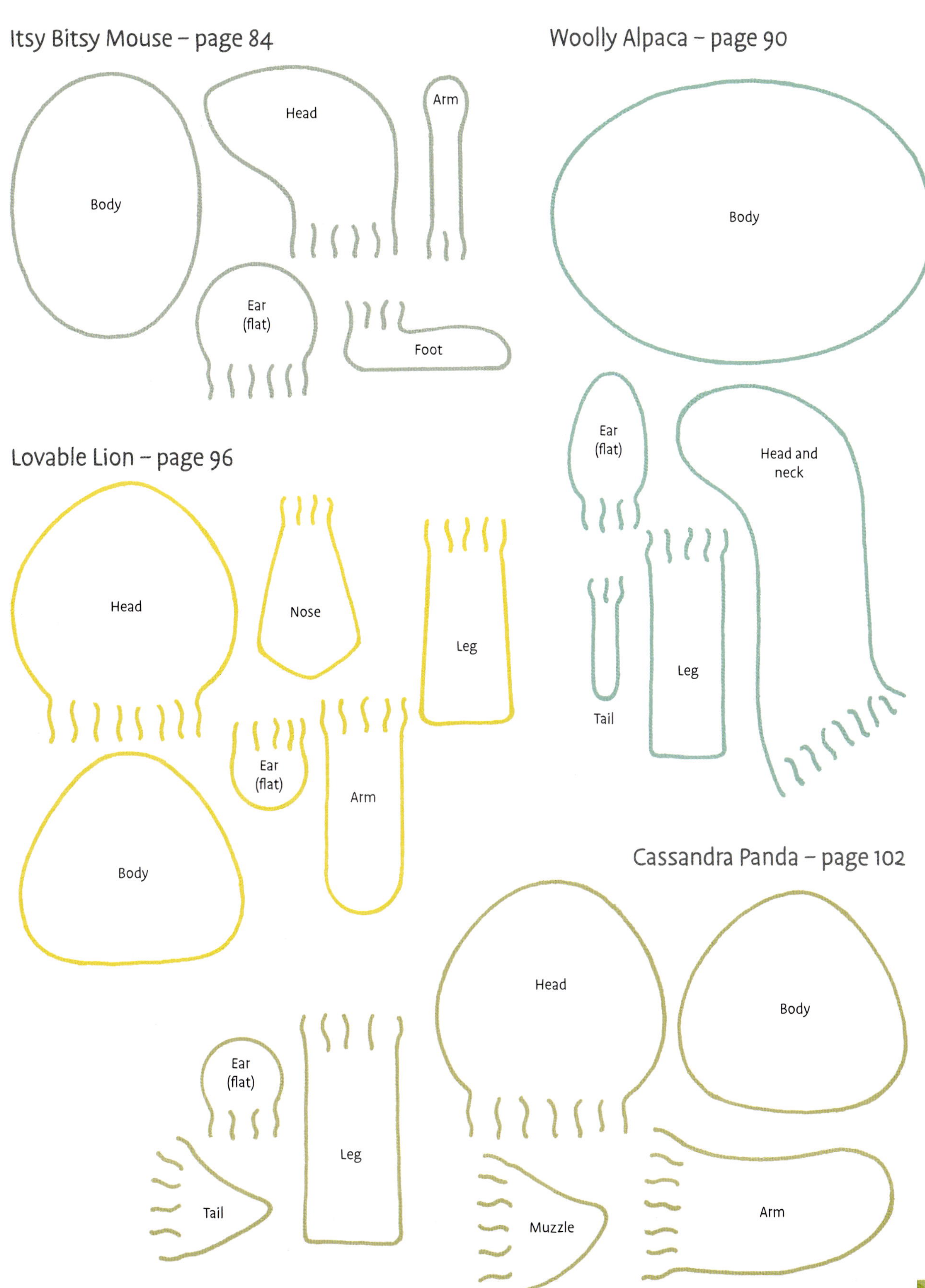

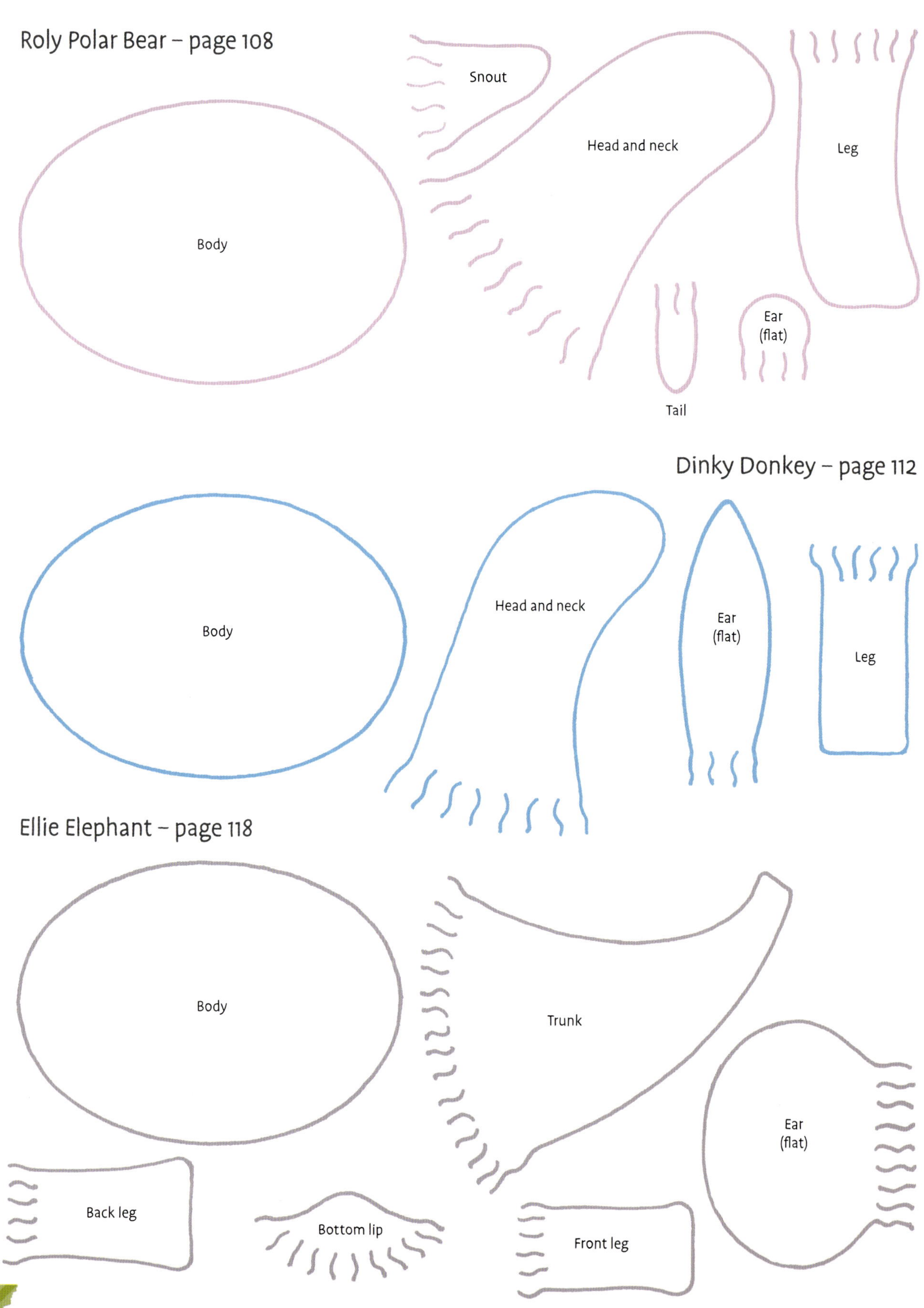

Roly Polar Bear – page 108
Body
Snout
Head and neck
Leg
Tail
Ear
(flat)
Dinky Donkey – page 112
Body
Head and neck
Ear
(flat)
Leg
Ellie Elephant – page 118
Body
Trunk
Ear
(flat)
Back leg
Bottom lip
Front leg

Gillian Giraffe – page 124

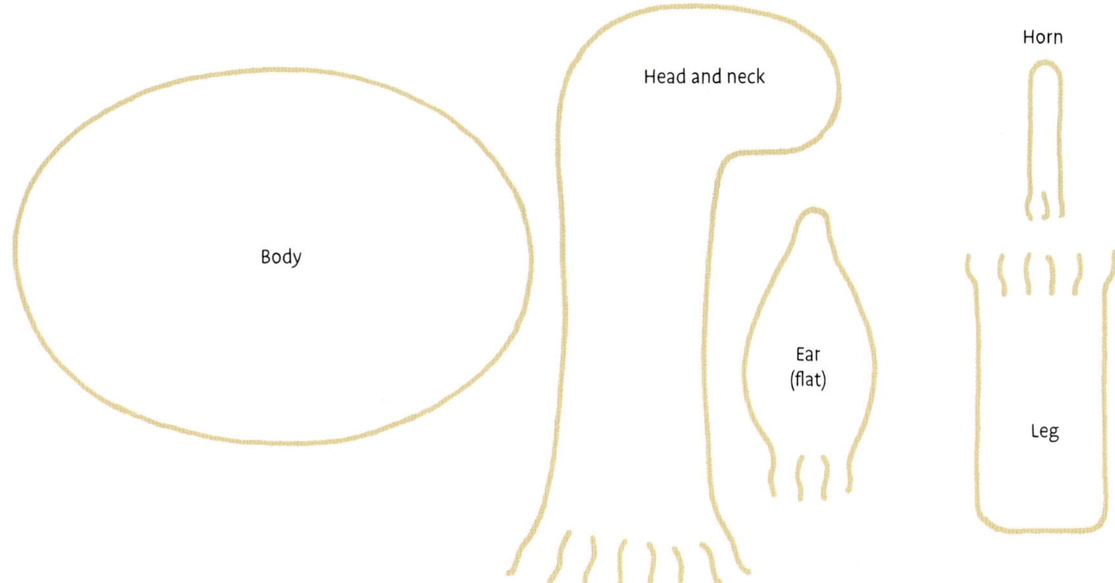

Cuddly Kangaroo – page 130

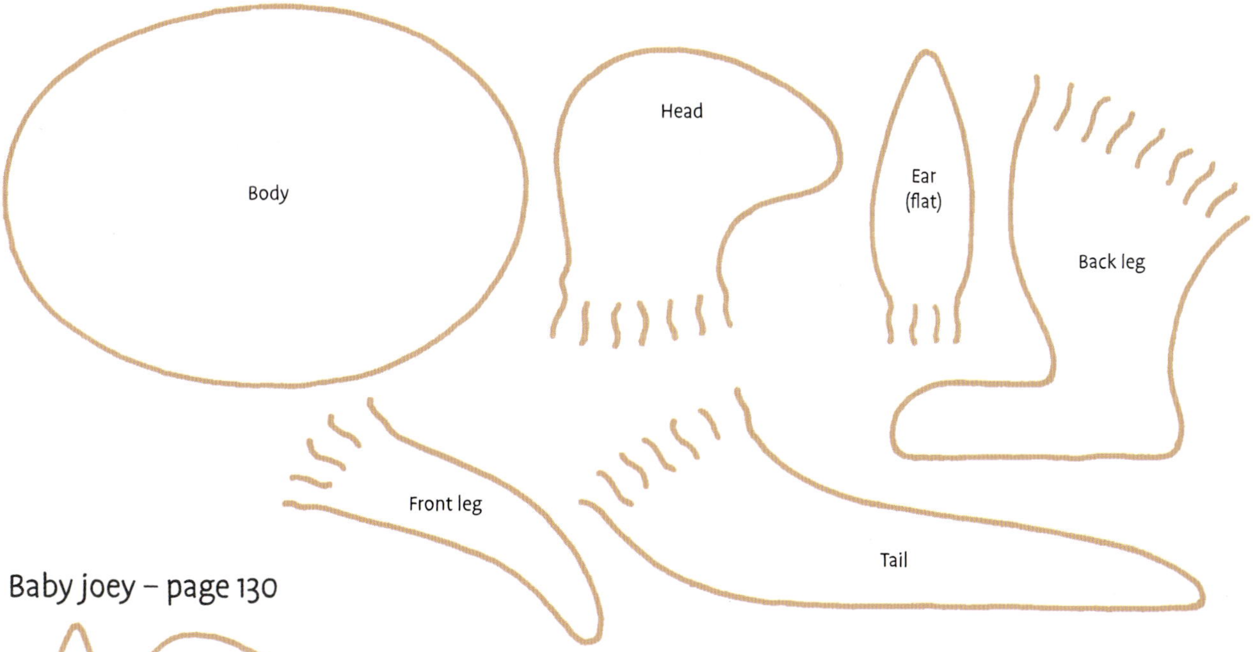

Baby joey – page 130

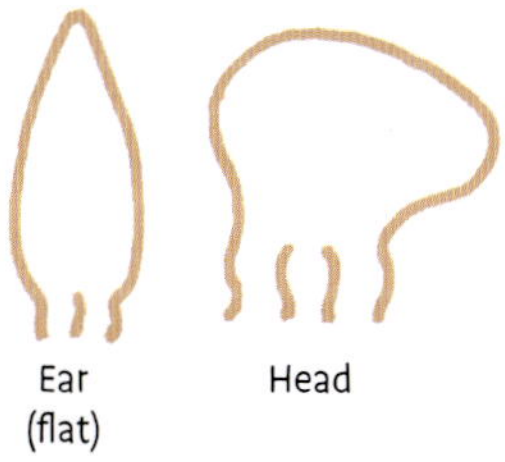

Index